LIFE BY SUICIDE

One mans journey to find happiness and salvation

By Michael F. Clark

AuthorHouse™
1663 Liberty Drive
Bloomington, IN 47403
www.authorhouse.com
Phone: 1-800-839-8640

© *2010 Michael F. Clark. All rights reserved.*

No part of this book may be reproduced, stored in a retrieval system, or transmitted by any means without the written permission of the author.

First published by AuthorHouse 1/26/2010

ISBN: 978-1-4490-5545-5 (e)
ISBN: 978-1-4490-5546-2 (sc)
ISBN: 978-1-4490-5547-9 (hc)

Library of Congress Control Number: 2009912725

Printed in the United States of America
Bloomington, Indiana

This book is printed on acid-free paper.

FOREWORD

This book is full of life saving information and was written for that purpose. There is nothing in this book that is not true. Neither is there anything that has been misrepresented. The stories containing my life experiences actually happened to me and are used to give you examples of Life by Suicide. My only wish and hope is that you receive something from this book that will help you reach your own level of seeking salvation. The bible verses are here for you to read for yourself and not take my word for it.

This is the story of one man's fight for his happiness and trying to find his salvation. It is because he had tried everything else that he could possibly think of, including suicide. Treatment centers after treatment centers, mental institutions and everything in between. This man could find no relieve in his life and therefore he created Life by Suicide.

This is his last line of defense in order to save his life. In this book is revealed some of the most hurtful and painful experiences that he went through. These things are only revealed because Life by Suicide calls for the brutal truth and no less. Life by Suicide is the last opportunity for this man to find happiness and salvation. Life by Suicide calls for the killing of ones self by ridding ones self of all the things that defile you. This is one mans journey. Today Michael died and yet Michael lives, this is Life by Suicide.

DEDICATIONS

I would like to first of all thank Almighty God, Jehovah for giving me life and guiding me through my writings. None of this would have been possible without his love for me and his will. Therefore all praise and glory goes to Jehovah God and his son Jesus Christ my Lord and savior. And it is through this that I was able to bring you Life by Suicide. Thank God for saving my life.

I would also like to thank my daughter Klasy K Clark, through some strength from God she was able to live through years of my addictions. And still managed to be a good child some how. And regardless of my problems she found it in her heart to continue to love me, even when I was unable to love myself. She went through everything that I did and even more. So today I would like to thank her for her understanding and love.

I would also like to dedicate this book to my little sister Cynthia Regina Clark, who was killed by a drunk driver on April the 16, 2004. She was just as great of writer as I am and did not get the full opportunity to release some of her writings and poems. So now she lives through my writings. May Almighty God bless her in the world to be!

Also I would like to dedicate this book to the only true friend I have ever had in my life, Lori Ann Lacy. Our friendship was one of true nature. She would always say to me that we will be friends until the end. And she was my friend to the end. Even on her death bed she was my friend, I had gotten myself in trouble and she knew it. I guess she could see the worry in my face or she just knew me that well. And when I should have been comforting her, she was worried about me. I said this is about the brutal truth, therefore this is what happened. I had used up my rent money on drugs two nights before. And when I went to visit her she asked me what was wrong. I told her not to worry about it. But she refused to let it go therefore I told her and she called her daughter into the bedroom where we were and told her to go to the bank and get rent money for me. She was my friend until the end and I love and miss her.

My daughter put it best in a poem that she wrote after Lori's death.

LOSING, LOST, GONE

LOSING, I am losing my ma. She was first diagnosed with cancer about a year ago. She was dying slowly, at the beginning she didn't change. but then she started getting bad stomach aches and she lost 35 pounds.

LOST, now my ma is lost. She doesn't know what she is doing, she can't walk. And she can't talk. She needs a diaper to control her bladder. We had the Pastor come by about 10 times, but it didn't work. God is good all the time. All the time God is good.

GONE, now my ma is gone. She died on November 22nd at 5; 33pm, the day before my birthday. My ma,

Lorrie Ann Lacy, gone out of our lives forever. What are we suppose to do? How am I going to survive?

Written by Klasy K Clark

Also I would like to dedicate this book to my long lost family that I now talk to often. Especially my mother, I thank God for her and to my brother's and sister's. May Almighty God continue to bless my family, for God knows that I have been the prodigal son!

Table of Contents

CHAPTER ONE
Committing Suicide 1

CHAPTER TWO
Pain, Suffering and the Truth 31

CHAPTER THREE
The Devil's Drug 53

CHAPTER FOUR
Michael's are Special 77

CHAPTER FIVE
Working and Fighting For Salvation 89

CHAPTER SIX
Having Accurate Knowledge 103

CHAPTER SEVEN
Who Am I Today 137

CHAPTER EIGHT
General Hates and Core Beliefs 157

CHAPTER NINE
My Last Words 175

CHAPTER ONE

Committing Suicide

It is nine days after my 50th birthday and I am tired. I am tired of everything and everyone; but mostly I am tired of me. I am not the person I dreamed I would be when I was a child. Neither am I the man, father, son, brother, uncle or person I want to be. I have wasted 50 years of precious life being **nothing** more than a space taker. I am tired of being uneducated, tired of my addictions; cocaine, alcohol, sex and food. I am also tired of the addiction of failure. My heart is so heavy with all of my dislikes, I should have done, what I wanted to do and what I needed to do. I am so sick of me that I don't even like me. The things that I want to do, I don't do. However, the things I don't want to do, I do. I sit on my toilet or in my recliner chair, or I go to my bed and cry to myself everyday. While there I come up with all the depressing things in my life and what I can do to change these things. Feeling motivated and yet I do nothing about it. Therefore the process starts all over again.

In March of 2008 I sat on my patio thinking of how tired I was and how disgusted I was with my life. There I watched the sun come up, it was one of the most beautiful sites I had ever seen or recognized. However, the sun looked at me and went back down below the skyline. It appeared to disappear amongst the clouds. At that very moment I knew that I was not the only person tired of me. I knew without any reasonable doubt that God was tired of me too. You might not understand this and I don't expect you to. However, I have had many interventions in my life by God or his angels. His only begotten son has been my mediator all of my life. From delivering newspapers when I was 11 or 12 years of age, I was preaching the word of God everyday. God has always been my heart and my whole life depends on God. The Bible was in my heart from birth, even in my mother's womb. I have never had any problems understanding the Bible; my problem comes from living by it. Today that is going to change.

Twenty-two years ago I woke up in a cold sweat, because of a dream I had. I woke up confused and scared because in this dream the devil and Almighty God was fighting over my soul. I was afraid, in pain, and feeling hopelessness; because this dream showed me that the devil had won. It scared me but I knew that God can never loose or be defeated. It was my own interpretation of the life style I had been living through my own subconscious mind, based on my guilt of how I had been living my life. God had nothing to do with it. However, God is still tired of me. You see when God brought me into this world and he had a plan for me, as he does for all of us. In my case God's freedom for me to choose the path of righteousness or wickedness, I choose the ways of this world and wickedness. God never left me or let me go. My pain and suffering got me to Life by Suicide. My God is a loving God. My God is love. However, because of me I have come to the conclusion that I must die in order for me to live. I have asked my God over and over again not to let me live anymore.

Please God, I have said don't allow me to wake up in the morning; only to wake up the next day. I've left legal papers so that my family would know my wishes. I've cried to God to let me die. Death has been a blessing to me for many years. I believe there are worse things in life and on this earth than death. I truly believe I would be better off if I was granted death. Gods love for me or his son's interventions has not allowed this to happen. Sometimes I say to myself, what is it that God want with me and why he won't grant my wish and prayers to die. What does God want me to do? Why is he letting me suffer? My life is full of pain and suffering and I don't want to be here anymore. I say with tears in my heart and suffering in my soul, please God I am tired. I desire dust in which I came from. However, it has not happened therefore I have decided to kill myself by committing suicide. Make no mistake this is the only way for me to ever live the life intended for me.

First of all I must start to take in poison in order for me to die. So you are about to read the death of a man killing himself while writing about it. Hopefully, by the time I finish this book I will be dead. Please know that I have received no professional help with the planning of my death; nor with the type of poison that I have chosen. The bible says; in order for a man to enter the kingdom of God he must be born again. I, truly want to be part of that kingdom therefore I will begin the process of my death by suicide. Once again make no mistake I truly plan on being dead to myself by the time I finish this book. Page four will be the beginning of my first dosage of poison. This is not easy for me and I never wanted it to come to this. But, I am truly tired of me and I have been left with no other real alternatives besides death. I, am tired of doing all the shameful things that I don't want to do; but yet I do.

People say that God will not forgive you for committing suicide. I have never read that in the Bible. One thing is for sure I will find out. Your prayers are welcome. I do know that there is no excuse for not knowing God, he has made himself known from the time the earth was created; please read Romans 1; 18-20. I, have been one of those persons failing to obey God and falling victim to this wicked system of things.

How does one commit suicide by killing himself and live after his death? Let me tell you a true story about an intervention in my life. I was on my way home from a friend's house as I was walking down the street about 9:00pm. I found myself wondering about my life and my future. I was about 19 years old, living in Atlanta, G.A. I, was feeling sorry for myself not having any family and living in a town with just myself, not knowing what was going to happen to me because I had left home 2 years earlier, because of my problems with my family. Please understand that sometimes in this book when I refer to leaving home I mean my immediate family and not my biological father's house. I was now feeling lonely, afraid, scared, hurt, and confused. I started talking to God about my feelings, not really praying but rather just talking. I found myself in what I like to call "inside a vision". God was responding to my conversation by showing me where I had come from and how far I still had to go. I, first saw the road behind me in which I had already traveled, which appeared to be of bright yellow and orange that had been mixed together to form a color, I have never seen before or after this inside a vision. I, then heard my spirit speaking to me about all the things I had done right and that God had approved of. But I also was told by my spirit the things that I had done wrong and about Gods disapproval of my behaviors. At this point in my inside a vision I began to recognize my purpose in life and how God had given me this purpose personally.

Having been already corrupt in my life; I was then shown the pain and suffering I would go through if I choose to disobey God and his purpose for me. Even though details were not included, my spirit realized the pain and suffering described. However, I was also shown that God would not let me fail no matter how long it took me to serve his purpose. Because like I stated earlier God can not lose, his word is final and can not return to him unfulfilled.

This is how a person can commit suicide and live after his death. A person must come to understand what it is in life they want and be willing to do whatever it takes to achieve it as long as it does not harm another human being. Let me tell you exactly what I mean by committing suicide and living after your death. First of all you have to be willing to take on the truth, which we will call poison. Why? Because the truth will set you free. You have to be willing to get rid of all those dark secrets that haunt you. You have to tell things about you that you have never told anybody in your life. Things that you cry about when you're alone. Things that dwell in your spirit, those things that make you shame of yourself without anyone knowing about them but you.

A person has to murder all things that defile God and are unacceptable to him. You have to rid yourself of hate, resentment, envy, lust, selfishness, toxic relationships, anger, evilness, lies, deception, and, wickedness, we have to murder all of these things and more. For some of us that means drugs, food, sex, gambling, the lust of money, and greed. Homosexuality and alcohol; being a workaholic, smoking cigarettes and weed because all of these things have killed our right to live. We must take our life back and the only way to do that is to murder ourselves within. You might ask yourself why I keep using the words murder, suicide and kill Well, if you are anything like me you already know why. But, for the sake of those who don't know here is a brief explanation. Have we not already tried everything from treatment centers to mental wards, we also even depressed ourselves being sick of ourselves. We have tried churches, we have moved from one place to another only to find out where ever you go there you are.

We have stayed in our homes hoping that something would change if we just stayed away from the rest of the world and people would just leave us alone. We have stayed in the bed all day hoping when we finally got up things would be different, we have been alone so we could be lonely, we have ate food to find hope, and used drugs, alcohol, gambling and all of our other addictions just to get away from ourselves. We have thought suicide over and over again. We have tried everything, you name it we have tried it. The one thing we have not tried is facing ourselves. We have not tried the brutal truth about ourselves; we have not released our secrets and admitted them. We have not confessed all of them. This is why we must consider the only option left to us and that is Life by Suicide. In the Bible, in the book of James 1;21 it says(so get rid of all the filth and evil in your lives and humbly accept the message God has planted in your hearts, for it is strong enough to save your soul). And after all is this not what we have been searching for; a saved soul, happiness, peace and the desire to love and to be loved. This was God's wish for us in the beginning; this was his plan for us all the time. We alone destroyed ourselves with our lust and desires of this world. Granted some of us have been victims and have been stuck on the wrong done to us, leaving us a mental and emotional wreck. But, we to can overcome the pain and suffering, by ridding ourselves of whatever was done to us and knowing that we were not at fault. And since this was God's will for us we have the authority to rid ourselves of all these great sins. Jesus Christ gave his life to free us from every kind of sin and to cleanse us from wickedness and wrong doing. It is our God given right to be happy and at peace with ourselves.

When we live our lives the way we have been, we are saying that our savior died in vain and that our faith in his death is weak. Do you not know that blood represent the proof of death? Therefore we need to bleed all of these great sins out of our lives in order for us to live.

My whole purpose for writing this book is to bleed all wickedness and sin out of my life. I, have tried everything I could think of to be happy. Nothing has worked for me. I, even tried suicide by cop; trying to get the police to kill me. I used as many drugs (crack) as I possibly could. I then went into a coroner store committed a robbery and waited for the cops to come and kill me. I, gave them every reason to shoot me dead; however it did not happen. It was not God's plan for me, his word cannot return to him unfulfilled. Therefore I lived another 30 years in my pain and suffering. I have been trying to escape from me for 36 out of the 50 years that I have been living. Sometimes I can just think of me and begin to cry, I am so unhappy with me. I wish for just one week of true happiness without having to use drugs or alcohol to make me feel good about myself. The fact of the matter is the only time I have ever been truly happy I was in prison. I am not talking about a happy moment; like having a child. I am talking about living in happiness for a length of time. Earlier I stated that I have never had any problems understanding the Bible, my problem comes from living by what the Bible says. I understand that we can never know happiness in its original state, our forefathers separated us from that when they disobeyed God and brought sin into this world and into our lives.

Unhappiness is a sin within itself. Anything that is not in agreement with God's purpose is a sin. God never wanted us to be unhappy. His plan for us was to be fruitful and multiply. His plan for us was to live forever without sickness and death. God wanted us to live forever. God looked at everything that he had made; saw that it was good very good. Read Genesis chapter one verses 28 through 31. God loved us so much that he gave his only begotten son, in order that everyone exercising faith in him might not be destroyed but have everlasting life; John 3; 16. Certainly he did not intend for us to live forever in an unhappy state of heart and mind. As a matter of fact God said in the book of Jeremiah 4; 4 (cleanse your mind and heart before the lord, or my anger will burn like an unquenchable fire because of all of your sins). This is more evidence that God wants us to be happy because he gets angry when our hearts and minds are not clean. It is not difficult to understand God's love and his devotion to us. Even in his creation of the earth his love was shown to us by creating everything we needed and wanted first, so that when ... created man, we would not want or need anything. He even gave us power over all that he had created and told us to be masters over it. For us to have subjection over the fish and flying creatures. And every living creature that is moving upon the earth. And to every wild beast of the earth. Every tree that bear fruit and every green thing our hearts desired we were to use as we saw fit.

You will see many Bible quotes throughout this book that is because in order for us to rid ourselves of all of the things that have kept us from living a happy and peaceful life, we must go to the source of our beginning. And, since God created us where else can we find his instructions for us besides the Bible. Now that we understand that we were not created to live in misery, we can move forward to committing suicide, so that we can finally live peaceful and happy lives.

Another word for Eden, where man was created is paradise or happiness. This is why every since God removed us from the Garden of Eden we have been unhappy and we have been searching for it every since. Therapy has not done us any good because we have to keep working on ourselves and taking medications that cause us more uncomfortable living. Counseling and every other kind of self help therapy from one on one to anonymous groups all force us to continue to relive our pain and suffering. So, that we never heal completely; because you have to work over and over on the same thing. Leaving a person to being happy for sometime just to return to unhappiness the next time you work on the same problem. Over and over we go through this process and never get better, no wonder we go to therapy year after year. Listen with your own heart and mind that God gave you and tell me if that makes any sense whatsoever. When a problem is solved it should no longer be a problem, because if it is; it has not been solved. Take responsibility for yourself and try to live the rest of your life by killing off all things that are indecent and sinful and that have kept you from being the person you want to be.

Now my approach Life by Suicide, teaches you to kill or murder these detestable things. To kill is an act to rid yourself of something that has caused you pain, just as it is when you commit murder.

Please don't confuse this thought with criminal activity, this is not our frame of mind. However suicide, murder and kill are all related to death. And when something is dead it no longer lives. It no longer has power over us, it no longer breathes, it no longer hears, nor is it any longer seen. It no longer feels, hurt or think. It is gone for all eternity never to be a force again. These things in our lives that have made us suffer need to be killed. They don't need to be worked on; they need to die forever so that we can live.

Have we not suffered enough? The Bible speaks of death in this matter "The living know that they are to die; but the dead no longer know anything" (Ecclesiastes 9; 5). Therefore, if we put to death the drugs, alcohol and the over eating, the hate, the anger, the resentments, and all other things that keep us dead to ourselves we can live.

This was not a part of this book when I first started to write it. However, it is now. It is November the 12th 2008 it is also 2:08am in the morning, and it is about thirty degrees outside right now. I used the term toxic relationships as one of the things we have to rid ourselves of. Someone whom I know just knocked on my door highly intoxicated with a five year old boy. My child and I were asleep at this time. It was the beating on my door that woke me up. This person stated to me that the child was her grandson and that she had been over her friends house drinking and wanted to enjoy herself, but couldn't. Because she had her grandson with her and that her daughter lives to far away to take him home at this time in the morning. She wanted me to wake up my daughter to see if she would babysit for her. I responded by asking her are you crazy, my daughter is asleep and has to go to school in the morning. Then this lady asked me if I would watch the child for her while she finished her drinking. I was shocked she had the nerves to ask me these questions at this time in the morning. I offered her and her grandson a place to sleep for the night; which she refused. I then told her she was wrong for walking around on the streets drunk with this five year old child at this time. She told me to go to hell and that if I was not going to watch her grandson then for me to get out her business. I told her if that's how you feel its fine with me and that they still could stay until in the morning. She told me to come lock my door, because she was leaving. As she was walking down my stairs I stood there watching, hoping I was doing the right thing for this child's sake. But, shortly thereafter I knew my hands were tied. Because this person to have a lot of demons in her life that needs to be killed in order for her to live. She also needs to commit suicide in order for her to live. I, know for a fact that she has been abused mentally and sexually both as a child and adult. Her life has been destroyed just like ours.

She has never gotten over the childhood abuse. And, it hurts so bad that she now uses alcohol and drugs to live with herself. In her mind this is the only way she can feel good about herself. If, I ever have the opportunity to speak with her in the near future I will offer my thoughts and help. I know that she to, is tired of being her. We have talked before so I know where she is coming from. If, not for the love of God there go I. She and I have talked about the Bible and our love for God many times however we have been trapped inside ourselves by our pain and suffering. We have been unable to get away from ourselves. Hopefully, I can reach back and help her once I help myself.

This is why we have to murder all that is within us that has caused us unhappiness. If, we were just quote; normal people we wouldn't have to use murder or suicide. But, we are not normal people we have carried our hate and unhappiness to long for any human resource to help us. We require help from only one source; God. We have to put everything in his hands. We have to confess to him so that he can forgive and heal us. He alone is the only source we have left nobody else can repair us. We have to go to the one and only person that have the power and authority to do whatever they chose. We no longer require temporary fixes; we require complete repair. Since God created us he is the only person that can truly repair us. He is the only person that knows how our hearts and minds work. We are the kind of people that must go directly to the source for our repair. Have you ever had a device or something that came with instructions to build or to put together, rather that something was a toy or entertainment center. And, you tried to put it together without reading the instructions. And it did not turn out the way it should have. Then you had to take it apart and start all over again only to read the instructions to get it to function right. This is where we are at this point in our lives. We can no longer take our car to a shade tree mechanic. We have to go straight to the dealership. For us God is the dealership. We need final and complete repair in order for us to function in our right capacity. Our true happiness can only be found if we take steps to fill our greatest need and that need is our hunger for spiritual truth and God's purpose for us. We are not drinking milk here we are strong enough for solid food. We have drunk all the milk we could and our lives have not gotten any better. We are now going straight to the source in order to fill our plates. We are going to live by committing suicide. We are going to God with the brutal truth. He knows all that we have done anyway, Therefore it is no need to feel ashame of anything. He already knows all of our secrets and all of our pain and suffering. And, guess what he still has allowed us to live. He loves us so much that he has waited for his children to come to him with all of their burdens.

God said in the book of Psalms, chapter 55 verse 22"throw your burdens upon God himself, and he will sustain you; he will not permit the godly to slip and fall". Regardless of how we think about ourselves and our past we have the opportunity to be forgiven. Then God will sustain you, if you simply ask. Speaking of the past I have lived on this earth with nobody to love and nobody to love me; but me. When I ran away from home at such a young age, I had no idea what I was getting myself into. My life has been nothing but pure straight hell since that moment. I have been to prison three times, in three different states. I have been locked up so many times I would not even try and count them. I, have been to treatment for drugs and alcohol at least 8 times. My DWI count is at least 13. I, have been shot, stabbed and beaten. I, have been hit in the head with a crow bar, I have participated in some very violent crimes against people and property. My life in mental illness centers for depression and thoughts of suicide is at least 11 by now. I am only happy or smiling when I have drank some alcohol or smoked some cocaine.

If, not intoxicated I am a very depressed and unhappy person. After all of my efforts to be happy, I have proven to be weak in efforts and accomplishments. I, try to quit all of these negative behaviors, only to repeat them all over again. Either I eventually give up or I allow someone from one of my toxic relationships (using people) to get me started all over again.

However, they are just as sick as I am; rather they know it or not. And, I am too weak to say no. People that are not addicted know nothing about addictions. They just have opinions based on what they believe or read, only a addict or a recovering addict truly knows what it is like and what needs to be done to recover. Nobody wants to live in the dark world of addiction. However, my addiction and the attempts to escape from it have lead me to Life by suicide. Not only in the scope of this book, but also in live generally.

On January the 8th 2009, I decided to become dead. How do you become dead? First of all I am a single parent, so I had to talk with my daughter about my plans. She has been with me all of her life; since she was 3 months old, she is now 16yrs old. My child has been through 16 yrs of my addiction and knows me like the back of her hand. She has seen my pain and suffering first hand and has also suffered through my depression. Actually, it's amazing that she has turned out to be the child that she is. My God heard my prayer's when she was first born. I was the one who cut the umbilical cord and washed the after birth off; along with shampooing her hair. After she received her immunization shoots I prayed to almighty God that he would raise her and that I would just be her caretaker. I told God that I was a recovering addict and ex- convict and knew nothing about being a father. I could by no means take care of this little girl without your complete help and support. And so far through all of my problems my little girl has turned out so far so good.

I explained to her how I felt and about my unhappiness as if she didn't already know. When you live with an addict of my caliber you become willing to do anything in order to have some peace. Therefore, when I told her what we needed to do, she was more than happy to comply. In her mind and heart that meant no more of my addict friends at the house. That meant to her that I would be stuck in the house, no liquor store, no drugs and even cigarettes was out the door. Because now that I am pretending to be dead I can't let anybody see me. The only problem I had with her through this process so far was staying off the telephone the day of my funeral. It is now January the 17th, 2009 and to ninety percent of people who know me believe that I am dead. It states on my answering machine that I died from a heart attack on January 8th and that my funeral is on the 17th. There is a note on my front and back door about my death and funeral. Only two people left messages of there sorrow. You might now be thinking that I was wrong for doing this, however you are not me. Did I not tell you earlier in this book that I was going to commit suicide in order for me to live? My life has driven me to this point. And, to be honest I am dead inside and have not lived in over thirty years; if not longer. However, there are a few people in my life that are not a part of my addictive life. Therefore, they know that I am not dead, plus these people have no contact or knowledge of my addict friends.

Also, people that I used drugs and alcohol with have never been my friends. Plus I have never been their friend. We use each other for drugs and alcohol only. We have never done anything together without drugs and alcohol. As a matter of fact if there is no drugs or alcohol there is, no us. When I call them or go see them it is in hopes that they have some drugs or alcohol and it's the same thing when they come see me. Now just in case some of these people really care about me and my daughter I have asked God to relieve them of some of their discomfort. However, I must do what I have to do in order for me to commit suicide so that I can live. Understand one thing before I go any further, I am tired of living my life around drugs and alcohol. Didn't I say earlier that I have tried everything that I could think of? So far nothing has worked therefore I will try death.

Now, pretending to be dead is a lot easier than you might think. First of all I have no family here, except my daughter. My funeral will be held in my home town, in which nobody knows anybody from my hometown that knows me. And as I said my addict friends will have a drink for me and a hit of crack and never think anything else about it. Once the word is completely out there no one will come by; nor will they call. Because now that I am dead, I don't have any drugs or alcohol for them; leaving them no reason to call or visit. Just to give you an example of what I'm talking about and how much these people care. One lady called about her fifteen dollars worth of food stamps that I owe her. I, guess she wants my daughter to give them to her if she get my food stamps next month. Yes, everyone in my life think that I am dead and I plan on keeping it that way until I complete Life By Suicide, because this is the only way for me to live. I have to let go of everything and everybody. If I forget where I come from on this I will surely go back to where I came from. And that is not an option for me. Once I kill every vile thing within myself I will not go back to the old me. I will be renewed in the lord and my hopes, dreams, prayers, actions, thoughts and thinking will be completely different. My desires will no longer be of things of the world that defiles me. My total reason for living is to do God's work. For that is the reason for life itself. Without God there would be no life. It is very important that God stay my number one priority in all of this, other wise I will fail again.

Some of us might not need to go to this extreme, I do. My concept of Life by Suicide can be based on the teachings of Jesus Christ, himself. However, this is a human concept and not a heavenly concept. Jesus told Nicodemus that unless you are born again you can never see the kingdom of God, (3; 3). Nicodemus, in return said; what do you mean. How can an old man go back into his mother's womb and be born again? Later on in that very same conversation Jesus said to Nicodemus, "you are a respected Jewish teacher, and yet you do not understand these things. If I tell you of earthly things and you do not understand, how will you understand heavenly things"? Hopefully we all now know that Jesus was not referring to a person literally entering their mother's womb again. He was referring to mankind changing their wicked ways and returning to the original state in which man was created. Jesus was talking about ridding ourselves of all of our sins. Those same things that keep us from being happy or entering the kingdom of God. Jesus was talking about ridding ourselves of hate, envy, lust, greed, and immoral sex, the love of money, idol worshipers, drunkards and addicts. Yes, Jesus was talking about homosexuality, jealousy, impure thoughts, eagerness for lustful desires, hostility, outburst of anger, selfishness, stealing, being unforgiving, the lack of love and etc.

Do not think for one moment that you will be allowed to do these things and still enter the kingdom of God. When I say or use the phrase kingdom of God I'm not talking about going to heaven I'm simply saying that you have an opportunity to live on earth in paradise. This was our original birth place. We must come to understand that we have been separated from our God through sin. Sin caused us to be the people that we are, not the people we were. That is why we have to be born again. Goodness and wickedness are not partners and never will be. How can goodness be a partner with wickedness? How can light live with darkness? What harmony is there between Christ and the devil? How can a believer be a partner of an unbeliever (2 Corinthians 6; 14-16). In the same way a sober man cannot be partners with a drunken man nor can a person that does not use drugs be a partner with someone who uses drugs. No more than a gambling addict can live in a casino or an overeater having lunch at an all you can eat diner. Opposites do not attract in that manner. So, Life by Suicide also teaches that the living can not be partners with the dead. Nor can you be born again or commit Life by Suicide while befriending unbeliever's. We must rid ourselves of all wrong doings and people that are causing us to live in wickedness.

Once a person rids himself of all that is evil and unrighteous he can be born again. He can live after he has committed suicide. The Bible says that once you are reborn you become a new person. That you are not the same any more, and that old person is gone from life. And a new life begins. (2 Corithians5;17). Life by Suicide is an opportunity to begin a new life and to be reunited with God.

I once was at a narcotics anonymous meeting and heard this guy say "I want to thank God for getting me to narcotics anonymous, and I want to thank narcotics anonymous for getting me to God". I didn't understand exactly want he meant, it literally did not make any sense to me. However, after carefully thinking about it, it made perfect sense. The gentleman was just simply saying if it was not for the other party I would have not been able to succeed. In, other words if God had not helped me get to narcotics anonymous I would have not been able to get clean off of drugs. And, if narcotics anonymous had not gotten me clean off of drugs, I would not have been able to find God. So, you see it's the same thing with Life by Suicide. If, I don't commit suicide I can't live and in order for me to live; I have to commit suicide. In the upcoming chapter I will begin to rid myself of all that I can think of that has held me back from living. Things that have held me back from God. The things that I told you are secrets. The things that I am ashame of, the things that haunt me, the things that make me cry when I think of them. The things I don't want to even think about when I am alone.

I, remember about twenty- two years ago when I was living in Portland, OR. This, woman who was a complete stranger, called out my name from behind. I, turned around to see who had called me and for what; because I really didn't know anybody from that city. Actually I was living in a homeless shelter. Anyway this lady told me my name, she told me not to worry about myself because I was not alone and that God had not forgotten me. She stated to me where I had come from, she said you have been remembered when you were a paperboy in Gary, In. She went on to tell me that I had come a very long way and that I had a very long way to go. This lady told me that after my pain and suffering I would return to God from which I came. I, asked her who are you and how do you know these things about me? However she just turned away from me and disappeared in the crowd. This was an event I have never forgotten in my life. This event has always come back and forth in my memories.

When leaving the hospital after the birth of my daughter. My daughter's mother was being wheel chaired out while I carried my daughter in my arms from the hospital; in Seattle, WA. This lady walked over to me and asked me to allow her to lay her hands on my daughter and bless her through prayer. I told her to step away from me and my child, that I know nothing about you. She said please sir allow me to bless your child, I told her no. And, I remember having an attitude about it "some strange woman talking about putting their hands on my daughter and praying. I didn't even know her; or who she would praying to". The reason I'm bringing this up is because for the first time in my life I just realized that the woman in Portland is the same woman in Seattle, some five years later. I have never thought about these two women in the same sentence in my life. Really, this has shocked me as I am writing this. I am actually amazed at this. But, now that this has been revealed to me as I am talking about it and as I am writing Right now is the very first revelation I have had of this connection between the two women. It was like it came out of nowhere. That, all of a sudden I realized

Michael F. Clark

that their voice, looks and physical appearance were all the same. I, now remember the hair style and the clothing they wore were all the same. They were the same height and weight.

I, need to take a break from writing in order for me to soak this in, because this has really given me something to think about. As, I told you, I have had many interventions in my life by a higher power. And, for me to just recognize this is strange. However, all praise and glory due to God because all things will be revealed in his time and not ours. My feelings about this, makes me feel blessed and honored that God has not forgotten me. Just twenty pages into my book God revealed to me, that he still loves me. And, that he has forgiven me of all my short comings. Do you have any idea what this means to me?

Just think about what I told you how I felt about myself from the beginning of this book. This revelation was an ego builder, it was a self- esteem booster, and it gave me hope and energy.

However, the down side to that is wondering if I missed a blessing for my daughter. That woman appeared to me twice in my life in two different places and times. Do you know that the Bible says," don't forget to show hospitality to strangers for some who have done this; have entertained angels without knowing it". It is my hope and prayers that I didn't turn an angel away from blessing my daughter. Also remember that I had asked God to take care of my daughter, because I did not know how. Some people don't believe that angels and interventions from heaven still take place on earth today. Well, I am not one of those people. I believe God is the same yesterday, as he is today and as he will be tomorrow. I believe God does not change nor does his plans. The only thing that changes with God is his prophets. And, that's just because man sinned and now can't live forever; until God's time. The Bible says in Hebrews 1; 12. But you are always the same, you will never grow old." The Bible also says in verse 14 that "but angels are only servants, they are spirits sent from God to care for those who will receive salvation." So for people to say anything different is not in harmony with the teachings of the Bible.

If, Satan, the devil; has demons in the world working to condemn man. Then you better believe that God has angels working to save mankind. After all God gave his only begotten son to make sure his plan and his word returned to him true. God created man to live forever. Adam's sin brought death; Jesus, death brought life. In the book of Romans 8; 38, 39 the Bible specifically says "and I am convinced that nothing can ever separate us from his love. Death can't, and life can't. The angels can't, and the demons can't. Our fears for today, our worries about tomorrow, and even the powers of hell can't keep God's love away. Whether we are high above the sky or in the deepest ocean, nothing in all creation will ever be able to separate us from the love of God that is revealed in Christ Jesus our lord". Whatever, the case may be, I am honored and blessed to be here today writing this book. Also you must know that I am after the brutal truth. This book is not to satisfy any religious belief or the right to believe. It is an attempt to save my life and anyone's life that wish to be reborn through ridding themselves of all wickedness. The Bible verses are here for your reference to make sure that I am telling you the truth. They are not here to give you something to debate about.

One of the very first things that personally separated me from God was my early age drinking. I am going to try and reach back over thirty years ago. All of this information is based on what I can remember and what I've heard over the years from my family. Keep in mind that there is 36 yrs, of alcohol involved here; so my mind might try to play tricks on me. However, the truth will be told. Let me say this first, even though we were born in sin because of our forefather. I believe that there is a point in our own lives where we personally separate ourselves from God. The reason I say that is because fresh out of our mother's womb we are innocent and have done no wrong. Our minds are in a pure don't know anything state. We are unable to decide right from wrong. We don't even know that we are naked. Sounds like somebody we know (Adam) the first man.

So when we are first born we are living in a temple of God's love for us. Just as God blew the breath of life into Adam and Adam became a living soul. It can also be said that once the doctor removes you from your mother's womb and slaps you on your rear end; you become a living soul. Now let's be reasonable, we all know that you have lived inside your mother's stomach for nine months totally depending on her. However, once removed you become an independent living soul, able to breathe on your own. So to use this as an example is not that far fetched. And, just as Adam lived free of sin so can we. It was only until Adam sinned that he separated himself from God. And so it is with us. Born in sin does not make you a sinner. You become a sinner when you sin. Even though we're more than likely to become sinners faster than Adam did. At what age we become sinners is to be determined seeing that sin is part of our nature now. You can even say that it is in our DNA and we have no other choice but to sin, at some point.

However, I believe that everybody separates themselves from God on a personal level as well. In other words you do something to set off your life of sin. For Adam it was the eating of the tree; in which God told him not to touch. For us it depends on each individual. I believe mine was drinking alcohol at such an early age. Because before that I was a mother's boy, if my mother was cooking I was right there with her. If she was in the basement sewing clothes I was right there with her. When I wasn't with her I was in my room reading my bible. I, need to correct something I said earlier about Adam not knowing he was naked. The bible does not say that. The Bible says "even through Adam and Eve were naked; they felt no shame". So rather they knew they were naked is another story, but it doesn't change our situation. Now being a mother's boy was fine with me because that's all I knew. It was my biological father that convinced my mother that if she did not stop me from hanging under her that I was going to be a sissy. My mother and step father disagreed with him, but after a while they decided I needed to have friends my own age. And, that I did need to get out of the house and go play.

After sitting on the front porch of my house crying day after day, because I couldn't go in the house with my mother or read my Bible; I left the porch. And, what I found up the street not even one block away was the beginning of my personal separation from God. I found a group of boy's some my age others older but it was obvious this was a gang. They were drinking alcohol, smoking weed, some were taking drugs, such as acid, they were smoking cigarettes and they had girls with them. But, the one thing they all had in common

Life By Suicide

was that they all appeared to be having fun. They seemed like they really cared for each other, they seem to have a connection with one another. They were all dressed alike and it appeared to me that there was order amongst them. These guys not only had everything above that I mentioned, they also had guns.

I remember the first time I saw a gun I was afraid of it, however I felt and knew the power a person had when holding a gun. Fortunately I never owned my own gun and I am glad I didn't. Later on one of my gang members would give me a stolen gun; which a dishonest police would later take from me to keep for himself. I remember that day like the back of my hand. I was in a night club, about the age of 19 yrs old. Sitting at the bar having a drink when this guy came to the bar and accidentally knocked me off my barstool. This guy was so drunk he could barely stand up. But, he had a mouth on him. He called me all sorts of names, plus he began to embarrass me with his threats of doing bodily harm to me. However I knew he was drunk and just talking trash. It was only until he said to me when you leave here I am going to blow your brains out your head, did I get pissed. At that point I got up off my bar stool and looked him straight in the eyes and didn't say a word to him. Keep in mind that I too had been drinking. The look I must have given him was of pure deadly hate; because at that very moment he began to apologize. However it was too late; I was ready to prove to him who I was.

Anyway I left the club to go outside to get my gun that I had hidden earlier. As soon as I picked up my gun a police officer came from behind me with his gun drawn. He ordered me to drop the gun which I did. I was then handcuffed, searched and checked for identification. The police asked where I had gotten the gun and if it was mine. I refused to answer any of his questions; he then told me that I had two choices. He said one I can take you and this gun to jail. And, two I can take off these handcuffs and you can walk away. I said, well what about my gun. He, said if this is your gun you are going to jail, however if this is my gun then you can go home. He then asked me what I wanted to do. I told him that I wanted to go home. He took the handcuffs off, and I walked away. This was not my first encounter with the police nor would it be my last. My drinking would keep me in contact with the law.

The gang that I was in favorite alcoholic drink was Richard's Wild Irish Rose Wine. Richard would be my master for many years to come. Even though I do not remember the first time I got drunk, I can tell you there were many of them. However I do remember this incident as clear as day.

A very good friend of mine and I had been drinking. We decided to drive from Gary, In. to Bloomington, In. We both had too much to drink to be driving such a long distant. As we were driving along, I obviously fell asleep and what woke me up was a voice. It was the most thunderous voice I had ever heard in my entire life. This voice carried with it power, it was a very demanding voice. It was commanding and the volume and the bass behind this voice was one of pure authority. It was the kind of voice that put fear in your heart. The voice was the kind that demanded instant respect and response. This voice made you react immediately without any delay, or time to think. This voice allowed no room for you to make a personal decision or form your own opinion. This voice was not just heard it was also felt. It left you no choice but to follow its demands. The voice said to me MICHAEL WAKE UP NOW. As I did I realized that we were traveling about 90 miles per hour. We were headed directly into a parked eighteen wheeler on the side of the expressway. My friend was sleep at the wheel and I had just enough time to snatch the steering wheel away from the truck ahead. We literally missed that parked truck by twenty five feet or less. My friend woke up after I lost control of the car from the violent jerk of the steering wheel.

Had not that voice called me when it did, we would have been killed instantly and on contact. I knew then as I know now, God had saved my life. My friend knew that God had saved his life after I told him what had happened. I rarely tell people about this incident, because it was private but mostly I got tired of arguing with people about their opinion. However, now I don't care what people think I'm trying to live my life doing God's will. Plus God deserves that glorification. I told my Bible study about it and other people who claim to know the Bible; only to hear that God does not talk to people like that anymore. I said it earlier and I will say it again. God does not change he is the same yesterday as he is today. People say to me that since you were drinking which God does not approve of drunkenness it was not God who intervened. However, from my understanding of the Bible Adam and Eve sinned against God when they ate the fruit that God told them not to eat. Yet, God clothed them because they felt ashame, (genesis 3; 21). Also, Cain killed Abel and yet after punishing Cain. Cain complained to God that his punishment is too hard; and that everyone seeing him will want to kill him. Then God told Cain that anyone doing harm to Cain, I will give them seven times your punishment, (Genesis 4; 15).So God has proven he will still protect us if he chooses, even after we have done wrong. Further proof of this is stated in the book of (Romans 9; 11) it clearly says "but before they were born, before they had done anything good or bad, she received a message from God. This message proves that God chooses according to his own plan, not according to our good or bad works". Jacob and Esau had not even been born when this message was sent. God also stated that (I loved Jacob; but Esau I rejected.

Now I am no more than a trying to recover drug addict. I am also an ex-convict, with a history of mental depression. I have sinned over and over in my life, I have also prayed for forgiveness. So people might think why would God love you in this manner? You are no prophet or person of great importance. I, don't know, ask God. I, do know that the bible say in the book of 1 Corinthians chapter one verses 27-30. "That instead God deliberately choose things the world considers foolish in order to shame those who think they are wise. And he chose those who are powerless to shame those who are powerful. God choose things despised by the world, things counted as nothing at all, and used them to bring to nothing what the world considered important, so that no one can ever boast in the presence of God". If you were to look at the book of Romans 9; 14 and 15 you will find that God said and I quote "I will show mercy to anyone I chose, and I will show compassion to any one I chose". I give thanks and praise to God for showing me his mercy and compassion.

BREAK TIME

I just witness live on television the Inauguration of Barack Obama. The first Black President of the United States of America. I am 50 years old and never thought I would live long enough to see this day. I was born in 1958, in Gary, Ind. and while a young man I remember the things that Black people went through in this country. I recall the images on TV and the voices on the radio. I remember the look on my parents face when Martin L. King was murdered. I recall the energy drained from the Black community from loosing one of our leaders. I recall the hurt and the pain. I remember saying to myself as a young Black boy, (I hate them white people).I am now 50 years old and living in Minneapolis, MN.

On December the 23rd of 2007 I was called a Nigger by the owner of a grocery store and told to get the "F" out the store. The hate and hurt returned, it was a reminder of how far we had truly come. Today I was reminded that, this was one mans hate and ignorance. And even though times have changed, we still have a long way to go. Racism and racial profiling is still alive and well. I do not want to go too far into this subject. I just wanted to recognize the progress we have made as a country. At the same time I want to confront the problems we still have. Without confrontation there can be no change. Therefore I truly hope that we can all take a look in the mirror and change what you see that is unrighteous. Let God's will take place in your life. While I have always been proud to be a Black man, for the first time in my life, I am proud to be an American.

Now let's return to the subject. My relationship with God is not on trail here and neither is the reason that God shows me mercy. What is on trail is my desire to rid myself of all that defiles me. My alcoholism has had a terrible effect on my life. It has help get me away from God and it has kept me from living a happy life. Alcohol is a mind altering drug to alcoholics. Some people can drink socially and never have a problem with when to quit. From the very moment that I started drinking alcohol it took over my life. It caused me problems at school, at home and it caused me to stop reading and studying my Bible. Alcohol was the main reason my troubled life got out of control. The Bible speaks about a drunk in this manner "don't be drunk with wine because that will ruin your life. Instead let the holy spirit fill and control you",(Ephesians 5;18). This Bible verse tells the story of my life. Because, alcohol help ruin my life. It started off with disobeying my parents and threatening to kill my father.

My family went to church every Sunday, Saturday night I was out late with my gang. We were drinking all night therefore Sunday morning I was in no shape to go to church. My father warned me three times to get out of bed and get ready for church. I never moved. Well the fourth time he came to get me out of bed. He had his belt with him. While still in bed under the covers my father hit me with his belt. And, all of a sudden I completely lost control. I started swearing at him and telling him that he was not my father and if he ever put his hands on me again I would kill him. I even went so far as to go outside and find a steel pipe and threaten to kill him if he came outside. This man loved me so much, everybody in the family knew that I was his favorite. The terrible thing about this was he was my step father. He also had two kids of his own that lived with us. And I was still his number one. I, loved this man with all of my heart. My father, Ted B. Goodlow I had broken his heart.

My mother told me that he forgave me long time ago because he truly loved me. However things were never the same after that. My heart and my conscious have never let me live that down. I, remember telling my father how sorry I was 13 years later. He did tell me he forgave me, but I didn't know how to take it; because we were at a bar drinking. I, never got another chance because my father passed away. Remember I talked about us personally separating ourselves from God, for me this was one of those moments. There was no honor in what I did. God gave us this command "honor your father and mother, and then you will live a long full life in the land that I will give you". This commandment was so important to God, that it is the only commandment with a promise. Now do you see how our personal choices can separate us from God?

This incident got me put out of the family home, and like I said it was due to my alcohol drinking. I would have never talked to my father like that had I not been drinking. Things are about to get a lot worse. With no alternative left I had to live with my biological father. I don't know if he loved me or not, but for the sake of fairness I will say that he did. However, I do know that my father did not want me there. I believe that he felt obligated based on the fact that he had not been a father to any of his kids. My father was also a man of hardship and had lived a very hard life. He had been to prison and had alcohol problems as well.

My father lived in the projects of Gary, Ind. His apartment was just enough room for one, plus my father was stuck in his ways. So to him I was more of an interruption than a son. I believe I was 15 or 16 years old at the time. I was able to go and come as I pleased. I was able to drink alcohol without any questions. As a matter of fact I drank alcohol with him many times. My father also bootlegged liquor on Sunday, so we were always drinking. He had two or three women who came over often and then it was time for me to leave.

Whatever, the case maybe our relationship was one of tolerance and liquor drinking. This would soon come to a head. One night while drinking together there was a disagreement between us. He started to raise his voice at me, and in return I did the same. This was not out of disrespect like it was with my step father. Because my biological father and I always swore with each other while we were drinking. That's just how our relationship was. However in his mind I guess I crossed the line and before I knew it he had his gun pointed at me. He then told me that he who blow my brains out my head if I ever talk to him like that again. I said daddy what's wrong with you. He responded by saying what kind of nigger are you and what kind of nigger do you think I am. It was then I truly saw the look in his eyes and I knew that my father actually could kill me. I now believe that he was tired of me being in his space because there was nothing out of the ordinary that happened. I believe that he wanted his old life back and didn't know how to be a father to me. He tried with all that he knew but it was not enough to him. I also believe that he was just an unhappy man, as I said that I am (like father like son) and he end up snapping. I know this to be a fact, now; because I see myself in him.

Sometimes my daughter has done nothing wrong and I snap on her because of my unhappiness. It was time for me to go, once again alcohol had separated me and another father.

At 16 years old I had no one now. After that I hated my father with a passion. And it wasn't so much that he had pulled a gun on me. Because, I had already been shoot by another gang. No, my hate came from the hate that I seen in his eyes for me. I had no doubt that my father would have killed me and I still have no doubt about it today. That day a tear fell out each one of my eyes and it took fifteen years or more before I would ever cry again.

This incident took place about 1976 and the next time I cried was 1991. I know this to be true because I was giving my wrap up in an impatient drug treatment center. A wrap up in treatment is when you are telling your story and you are about to graduate or move to the next phase. This treatment center was for a full year. I had been there 9 months and for the first time in my life I felt hope. Tears came from everywhere, running down my face like a water fall. Fifteen years or more of pain and suffering came out all at one time. There had to be sixty people I was standing in front of crying like a baby. I cried so hard and so long almost everybody in the room was crying, including the men. I thought I had finally gotten rid of myself, after nine months of nothing but treatment, everyday all day. It was not to be, because here I am. I look like my father, and he looked like me. We both have been to prison, we both are alcoholics and we both were very unhappy people. He also has pasted away and to me that just meant another father out of my life that left with no chance to ask for forgiveness or to say goodbye. Alcohol was ruining my life, it had already taken two fathers and my family.

At 16 years old I felt defeated with no hope. With nobody to love and nobody to love me; but me. The Bible was telling the truth alcohol will ruin your life (Ephesians 5;18). However, my hate for my father burned in my mind and soul for many years to come. Even at his funeral, when I viewed his body I was swearing at him in my mind. I even answered the question he asked me the night he pulled his gun on me. I told him that I am a living nigger and you are a dead nigger. I don't believe anybody in my family had any idea what was going on in my heart and mind at the time. This painful event still hurts me today and that's why tears are running down my face right now. This is one of the reasons I must commit suicide. This is one of those things that have haunted me for to long. This is one of those things that I cry about whenever I think about it. Proverbs 23; 21 says "for a drunkard and a glutton will come to poverty and drowsiness will clothe one with mere rags". The content in which this is used is to show the outcome of my alcoholism. Poverty represents the failure of life and drowsiness meaning I don't know where to go or what to do. Clothed in mere rags mean my life is unmanageable.

However, I grew up later in life and forgave my father. I guess the reason I still cry about it, is I have not forgiven myself. However I am committing suicide right now and getting rid of everything that hurts. This incident is about to be murdered. It will have no more life and it will no longer breathe the life out of me. My alcoholism allowed me to hold on to this hate and unforgiving attitude for to long. Before I go any further you need to understand something.

Life by Suicide is not just revealing your pain and suffering through your admission of guilt, thought, emotions, and feelings. It also involves a lot of prayer and praising God. It causes you as well to give glorification to God after you have revealed your hate. God requires thanks for giving you the strength to confront your life. Life by Suicide calls for you to read and study the bible; because this is where our creator left his instructions how to live our lives. For some of us it calls for fasting as well. This is my story, so remember to use your pain and suffering. And don't be afraid of the brutal truth .The truth is the only thing that will release us of our secrets. And our secrets are the only thing that will release us from our pain and suffering. So be completely honest and let go of your secrets. I would like to say at this point that I have forgiven my father. Life by Suicide also calls for us to forgive others for the wrong they have caused us. How can we expect God to forgive us if we are unwilling to forgive others?

I use to hold grudges for years, I mean everything that somebody did to me I kept in my heart and mind. I could hold a grudge for twenty years and hold on to the hate and emotions of that grudge. To this day I can remember 98% of everything and everybody that I felt did me wrong. I do not think about it as much as I use to, but I still remember them.

These grudges turn into resentments that cause irrational thinking. This thinking comes out in all different kind of forms. And sometimes little things that really don't mean much can cause you to over react. All based on that hidden resentment that you have not let go of. You sometimes take your anger out on people or situations that don't deserve it. Good nurturing people have the tendency not to want to be around people that drain them of their positive energy. And people like us loose a lot of good relationships with our deep hidden resentment. God blessed me with an experience that changed my thinking and life about forgiveness.

I was in King County Jail in Seattle WA. waiting to go to prison for some arm robbery charges. I had already been to court and was found guilty and I had already been sentenced. One Sunday the guards announced over the intercom if anyone wanted to go to church services. I decided to go and I did. Once I arrived in the jails church, I realized that I was the only inmate there. The only other people there was this older married couple, we had church service. The following Sunday the same thing happened again. It appeared to me as well as this couple that it was just us three once again. However we still had church service. The next Sunday I attended church again only to see the same couple the previous two Sundays. Before we started church service they asked me if I remembered them. I told them of course I do, you guys were here the last two Sundays. They then said, no; do you remember us before then. I told them no and that they must have me confused with someone else. They then stated to me do you remember robbing us at so and so store (I will not use the name of the store).

Once they said that to me and I took a good look at them my head just fell on the table. I did remember robbing them. Now I'm in jail with a three year sentence to serve in prison only to meet victims of a crime, I had not been caught for. I have now been identified by two other people that I have robbed. Plus I'm in jail and can't go anywhere. I have singed my name on the church list three times with my jail ID number. My heart sunk to the floor, because now once these people report to the authority that I robbed them. That meant to me another four or five years that I would have to serve in prison. We did not have service that Sunday, instead they talked to me about my crime against them. They told me that they had forgiven me a long time ago and they had no intentions on telling or reporting this to the authorities. Of course I did not believe them. When church services were over and the guards came to get me, I was already convinced that they were going to say something; they didn't. All that next week I was stressed out just waiting until the guards came to me to serve me papers on this new arm robbery.

The next Sunday I did not go to church. However, because they were prison ministers they could visit inmates anytime they chose. Later that same Sunday the guards called my name and told me I had visitors. It was the couple that I was trying to avoid. They asked me why I did not come to church today. I told them I was afraid because I knew they were going to tell. They said to me, Michael; we are Christians and we told you that we would not report you to the authorities and we will not. They showed me scriptures in the Bible about forgiving others. Matthews 6;14,15 says " for if you forgive men their trespasses, your heavenly father will also forgive you. Whereas if you don't forgive men and their trespasses, neither will your father; forgive your trespasses". Plus they told me what an honor and blessing that God had bestowed upon them by having the opportunity to minister to someone that had wronged them. They said that this was not by accident that they had met me in jail. They said this was God's plan for them and for me and they would not loose this opportunity.

At that point I believed them. They came to visit and minister to me two to three times a week. When I was sent to prison they traveled 75 miles each way every week to see me. They left money on my jail account for me to buy the things I needed. They brought clothes for me to wear all while they prayed for me. They continued to befriend me and I them. The day I was released from prison I was sent to a one year impatient treatment center for drugs and alcohol. I mentioned this earlier. They went through that whole year with me, they were there when I cried like a baby. Upon my discharge from treatment I was invited to their family home where I met their entire family. They cosigned for me my first apartment. When my daughter was born they were waiting outside the delivery room. They also became my daughter's god parents. The Bible says in Jeremiah 31; 34" for I shall forgive their error, and their sins I shall remember no more".I had never seen or heard of that kind of forgiveness in my life before. And yet I lived it. The love they had for people and the love they had for God changed my life. I thank God for the pleasure of meeting and knowing these people. They pasted away doing God's will; prison ministry, Hebrews 13;3 " keep in mind those in prison bonds as though you have been bound with them. And those being ill treated, since you yourself also are still in body.

This experience gave me the ability to forgive and to let go of any grudges that I ever had. I learned to release resentments and though I am still in body I have the ability to remember the grace shown to me anytime I'm wronged. And anytime I struggle with forgiving somebody as soon as I remember and reflect on this incident, I forget immediately. And I praise almighty God for that. All glory is his and his alone. How could I not be forgiving after that experience. God had once again intervened in my life in hopes of saving me from myself.

CHAPTER TWO
Pain, Suffering and the Truth

I will go back to alcohol being one of the things that personally separated me from God. But first I want to get this out of my way. I've told you over and over about the brutal truth. And what I am about to talk about is very hurtful and painful for me. However it is the brutal truth, and if I don't get this out now I might not do it at all. Life by Suicide in my case would not be completed, and neither can I ask God to forgive me; if I am unwilling to confess. How can I ask God to bless my writing if I don't reveal all? Furthermore how can I show you the way if I don't go with you. This, incident also help personally separate me from God.

When I was 13 or 15 years old a friend and I had been drinking. We wanted to go to this night club and get something else to drink. However, we had no money. While we were trying to get some money a car pulled up to us and asked us if we wanted to make some money. It was two homosexuals that waned to perform oral sex on me and my friend. We told them no. However, they circled the block and my friend and I talked about it and we allowed them to do it; for forty dollars a piece. I knew the moment that, that act was over I had drained more God out of me. I have never been more shameful of anything in my life. I know how much God hates homosexual activity. My life would take a drastic turn for the worse. While all sin is sin in God's eyes, there are sins that are more serious. In the book of Exodus when the men of Sodom went to Lot's home to have sex with the two men that had just arrived in town. Lot told them no, however I do have two daughters that have never been with men. Please take them and do whatever you want. The men of the city said no we want the visitors. The two men were actually angels. Therefore they blinded the men of the city and told Lot to get all of his family and get out of the city. Lot was taking to long so the two angels grabbed Lot and his family and took them out the city themselves. They also told Lot and his family to flee to the mountains and don't stop anywhere. They told him not to even look back. And Sodom was completely destroyed the next morning. I told you that story for this reason. Homosexuality is so hated by God that out of the nine hundred to one thousand or more pages in the Bible; which are all double pages. He placed his dislike for homosexuality on page 27. God was so angry that he wasted no time in the destruction of that city. God hated this act so much that he gave them up to sinful thoughts.

The Bible says" those who indulge in sexual sin, who are idol worshipers adulterers male prostitutes, homosexuals, thieves, greedy people, drunkards, abusers, and swindlers, none of these will have a share in the kingdom of God"(1corithians 6; 9,10). God does not like sexual sins. This is the reason God flooded the earth the first time. In chapter 6 of the Bible book Genesis verse 1 it says "now it came about that when men started to grow in numbers on the surface of the ground and daughters were born to them. Then the sons of the (true) God began to notice the daughters of men that they were good looking, and they started taking wives for themselves". Later in verse 6 and 7 God said "and God felt regret that he had even made man in the earth and he felt hurt in his heart. So God said" I am going to wipe men whom I have created off the face of the earth". So you can clearly see God's displeasure with sex sins and homosexual sins. Besides disobedience the only other great sin that had been committed was murder when Cain killed Abel. This is one of the reasons God gave up men to the desires of their own minds and desires of this world. He intentionally closed their minds for them to go and do whatever shameful things their hearts desired.

And as a result they did vile and degrading things with each others body. Even women gave up the natural use to have sex with men; and started having sex with each other. And the man instead of having natural relations with women engaged to having sex with each other. So men did shameful things with each other and suffered within themselves the penalty they so richly deserved. As for me my heart was broken, and it took me a long time before I was able to ask God to forgive me. I was shamed to my very core. There were times I could not even bow my head in an attempt to pray. Somewhere down the line of life I was able to go to God with a humble and repenting heart and ask for forgiveness. However we are talking years later before that happened, during that time I was on my own. I had no godly conscious or godly fear.

However this was a one time act for me. I soon found my love for God and was able to remember all the different scriptures I had read as a paperboy. This alone gave me the strength to recover from my wickedness. I remembered that if I would confess with my mouth and believe in my heart that Jesus was raised from the dead, I would be saved. I remembered that the Bible said that all men have sinned and fall short of the glory of God. That no one is good. But the thing that made me know that God had forgiven me was I remembered that because of Jesus Christ dying for me. I could be saved regardless who I was or what I had done. And, that God would not even remember my sin anymore once he had forgiven me. Being separated from God like that put the desire in me to never commit such a sin ever again. I didn't care what I would ever do I knew that I would never hurt God like that again.

You have to have a relationship with God to know and feel that you have hurt him. I was only 13 or 15 years old, but I had been reading my Bible as a mother's boy for many years before that act. Therefore I had something to go back to. Rather a person knows it or not you can not hide any thing from God. The day will come when God, by Jesus Christ will judge everyone's secret life.

In today's world homosexuality has been accepted. However it is wrong in God's eyes. Even churches have approved of it and some states allow same sex marriages. Listen this is not the purpose of this book to get into political issues concerning this world. However, it is my right to stand up for what the one and only true God has said through his book the Bible.

This was a sin I committed and I paid for it. Some sins we commit we can only commit that one time because something worse might happen if you do it again. For me that act of homosexual participation was that sin. It has never happened again. Do you remember when the religious leaders and Pharisees brought a woman to Jesus and said this woman was caught in the act of adultery. And the Law of Moses says to stone her. And, Jesus told them, he who has not sinned, throw the first stone. He then turned to the woman and said, where are your accusers? Didn't even one of them condemn you, no; the woman said and Jesus said well neither do I, now go and sin no more. Also in John 5;14 the Bible said that Jesus told a man that " now that you are well go and sin no more, or something worse might happen to you". It is my belief that some sins are worse than others. The Bible says" I can't believe the report about the sexual immortality going on amongst you something so evil, that the pagans don't even do it". Sexual sins are one of the very few sins that a man can commit against his own body. And the body is the temple of the Holy Spirit, which lives within you, and was given to you by God. So run away from sexual sin! No other sin so, eagerly affects the body as this one does.

Now that I have gotten that painful experience down on paper, we can continue with the drunkenness in my life. One thing more the reason not much time was spent on the above topic. Was that it happened one time and it has not affected my life except for how I spoke of it. Therefore the time spent was appropriate and not because I did not want to face it.

Now alcohol has affected my life for over thirty six years. It has caused me more pain and suffering than anything else. It has kept me separated from God and every other good thing in my life. As a matter of fact I would have never made the decision to participate in a homosexual activity if I had not been drinking. So Life by Suicide for me must associate itself around alcohol. Alcohol is at the very beginning of all of my problems. It all started to go down hill for me the moment I had my first drink. You might have different problems, that personally separate you from God and that would be what you would focus on to commit suicide. Remember we are after those things that have caused us pain and suffering all of these years. Things we are shameful of, things that make us cry, the things that hold us back from being ourselves. So whatever that is for you rather it be alcohol, gambling, overeating, homosexuality, envy, or hate it does not matter, you know what has held you back and forced you to live an unhappy and painful life.

Once alcohol had taken my entire family I decided to join the military. The one and only place I would be accepted. My anger and hate for life had turned me into a person looking to hurt someone or something. I could even see myself killing another human being. Yes! The military was the perfect place for me. I finally began to fell good about myself again. I could get away from my gang and my family all at the same time. Therefore I went to the recruiting office downtown Gary, Ind. and filled out an application for the military. I truly don't remember rather I was old enough or not. Either way it didn't matter because I could always get one of my parents to lie about my age. As many problems that I had caused them I knew it would not be a problem. So I took the test they offered me. After passing all of my preliminary tests I was going to Chicago, for further testing and physicals. There I passed all my tests and physicals the only thing left for me to do was to be sworn in as a member of the United States military.

However there was a five hour waiting period before I had to swear in. I met another guy in the military lunching area and we decided to have a drink since we both had at least five hours before we had to swear in. And the last thing that I remember is standing downtown Chicago in the alley drinking one hundred proof Old Grand Daddy whiskey.

When I woke up I was in a locked room on a cot. There was no one else around. However shortly after I had awoken two men in full military uniforms came into the room and told me to get up. I tried to question them about my whereabouts they told me I would find out in a moment. I was then led to an officer's office who told me that I would never ever be allowed in the military. I had apparently cursed out several officers and interrupted the swearing in ceremony by talking about how much I hate white people. I was told that I had said that they murder Martin L King. And that I would never fight for this country the way you have enslaved my people. I was given a permanent discharge and was escorted off the property. Actually I don't truly recall what kind of discharge I was given, seeing that I had not yet sworn in, but I do recall the officer giving me some type of paper work and telling me that I would never be allowed in the United States military. Yes! My old friend and only associate alcohol had done it to me again. It seemed like alcohol wanted to have a relationship with me and didn't want anybody else in my life. I did not even mention all the schools I was put out of because of my drinking. I was enrolled in one school for forty five minutes before the principle called me to his office. He told me that he had no idea how I got into his school but looking at my record I was not going to stay. I was escorted out of the school before I had done anything wrong.

I remember going to a concert only to remember nothing. I remember giving my concert ticket to enter the concert hall and when I woke up the concert was over. The stage was empty and everyone else was gone. I didn't see or hear anything during that full concert. Actually I had to break a window to get out the building. I couldn't believe that through all that noise and thousands of people screaming at a concert I did not remember anything except going in. Yes sir, the Bible was right, when it said" don't be drunk with wine because that would ruin your life" (Ephesians 5; 18). It was definitely telling the truth in my life.

However at the time I had not figured it out yet. Because in my mind there were other reasons my life was so bad and yet none of them had to do with alcohol. In my mind my parents did not love me and that's why they put me out of their home. I had a lot of resentments against my family and found myself in this world all alone. From the age of 16 to fifty years of age I have not lived with my family. I tried once before when my daughter was born. But my anger and resentments were still alive and well. So even after decades my feelings had not changed due to the fact I had done nothing to change them.

I thought that since we had not been around each other for so many years things would be different. That was not to be the case. I can't say that it was any body's fault. We just had unresolved issues that had never been confronted. Mostly I had unresolved issues because I never released any anger at that time in my life. I held on to hate and resentments like I held on to alcohol. Nothing was ever my fault. And if it was it was only because you did something to me and that's why I did what I did to you. Anyway my journey alone in life continued. This is another reason I have to commit suicide. Why should I live the rest of my life without my family? I've always missed them and wanted to go home but just never felt wanted or needed. I always had that anger that would make me say to myself I'll show them. There were many of nights and days I wanted to call home but I never did. My life was one of loneliness and selfishness.

Selfishness is another reason we have to commit suicide. Anyone that has a major addiction is selfish. Part of that addiction is selfishness. When a person does something over and over knowing that it is causing problems and they continue to do it regardless of the outcome; that's selfish.

All addicts hurt themselves and people around them. The selfishness comes in to play when you continue to do it knowing that you are not only hurting yourself but also your love ones. When we continue our addiction regardless of our surrounding we prove that nothing is important except us. I can't even count the times I've put my addiction in front of my rent, food, light and gas bills. I've even put my addiction in front of my daughter and her needs. Praise almighty God that he remembered my prayer asking him to raise her because I was incapable. Alcohol has even stopped me from being the good father that I could have been. I fought hard and long to get custody of my daughter because at the time I was the better parent. No questions asked! My daughter's mother was in no shape whatsoever to take care of our child. It was therefore my responsibility, and not the grandparents and I accepted that responsibility without a second thought.

Plus I never wanted another man raising my child, holding her in his arms. Teaching her what he believed in. My selfishness through my addiction has gotten in the way of that also. I know from any reasonable doubt that no one wants to be in the grasp of addiction. People that are not addicts think that it is a choice and that if a person really wanted to quit they would. These people lack any knowledge about true addiction. I can say this because I am living it and I have lived in it, around it, with it, through it, for it and over it. People believe that addicts are weak and lack strength to will themselves out of their pain. They say if we as addicts had the will power that we could quit if we wanted to. They say that people that have a problem just need to stop.

I remember when they came out with this" just say no" campaign. That worked out real well, did not. Then they came out with hard core behavioral modification programs that really worked; did not. Then shock treatment, then 21 days of impatient treatment, nothing these people have tried has yet to stop addiction.

I know people that had over twenty years of sobriety only to return to their old addiction. I myself have tried everything possible including acupuncture. I told you earlier how many treatment centers I have been in. None of those things worked for me for any long length of time. I know for some people they do work. But for this addict they don't. My addiction is deeply embedded in my spirit. It is not some sort of virus that can be treated with these temporary fixes. I need to be reborn. I need to start from a point of complete nakedness. I need to have the blessing of almighty God in order for me to recover. I have to recognize God, not just say my higher power. I am so far gone I need to give that power complete acknowledgment.

People around me think that I am a good father or doing the best that I can. And that might be true to them, however I know I am a much better person than I have shown to be. Also the people that think that are just as sick as I am. They are looking at goodness through sick eyes. My own spirit tells me that I'm not the best that I can be.

Alcohol is the foundation of my wickedness and it has a lot of other symptoms with it. These symptoms must be identified in order to confront them. That's the only reason I brought selfishness into the picture, it is one of the symptoms of addiction. No addict can deny the selfishness involved with addiction. It is one of the driving forces behind the need to be happy. Happiness is about me, and me is about self. Selfish is defined in the dictionary as "taking care of ones self, without regards for others".

When I received my last DWI, I had no idea where my daughter was. I was convinced that my daughter was in the back seat of the car. I complained to the officers in jail that when I was arrested my three year old child was in the car when they towed it.

Officers in the jail house could care less about how you got there, less known some wild story. They have heard some of everything during their years of working in jails. Therefore it took me at least one hour to get an officer to even listen to me. The officer took me to a room and listened to my story and told me that she would call around to find out where my car had been towed. And then she would call the tow yard and have them check to see if there was a child in the back seat sleep under the cover. After about forty five minutes she came and told me to relax. That they had found my car and there was nobody in the back seat. While I was overjoyed I still had no idea where my child was. I was released three days later and I still had no idea where my child was.

Immediately I started to wreck my brain as to where my child was. The last thing that I remember was picking her up from day care after I got off from work. I also remembered stopping at the liquor store. And that is all that I recalled. After calming down I decided to call my babysitter to see if I had left her over there. Thank almighty God that's where she was. I had apparently dropped her off earlier that day. I was so selfish that I went to go get a drink to calm down. My selfishness caused me to come to the conclusion that I didn't need to drink and drive anymore. Therefore I stopped driving it never crossed my mind that I needed to stop drinking until years later. Almost every single parent in this world should have transportation in case of an emergency with their child.

My selfishness has never allowed me to even to go to the department of motor vehicles and apply for a driver's license. That's right I am fifty years old and have never applied for a driver's license. With my addictions of alcohol and selfishness I don't even know what my blood type is. It has never been a concern to me. This is what I meant when I said that selfishness is one of the driving forces to being unhappy. How could a person live fifty years and not be concerned or even know what their blood type is. As I sit here today writing if I were in need of blood I would not be able to tell the doctors what my blood type is. It seems that things that are important to other people they are not that important to addicts. I can't count the times that I put my addiction in front of everything except my addiction. That means if we needed food and all I had was twenty dollars. I thought about how much my addiction would need and then what was left over I brought food. My selfishness has left out all and everything important to me except my addiction.

This is why suicide is the only alternative left for me. If I don't kill myself I will not ever be able to live a life of happiness. I told you that I have tried everything except the murder of myself. I have for the last several years tried to come up with a way to rid me of myself. And the only thing that came into mind was death however, I do want to live. Therefore the concept of Life by Suicide was born. My reading of the bible in order for a man to enter the kingdom of God he must be born again. This was what I needed and it made perfect sense to me. What did not make sense to me was treatment center number 8, or mental clinic number 11.

The last time I went to treatment for my addictions they wanted me to place my child in child protection services and give up my apartment to go out of state to a 90 day clean and sober house. They told me that if I wanted to get sober that I would have to be willing to go to any length. I knew that what they were telling me was true for somebody else, but not for me. Even if it was an alternative for me it made no sense to me. I explained to them that I have been to prison three times. And to treatment at least seven times and you want me to put my child in child protection services, in hopes that since she was placed voluntarily I would have no problem getting her back. And you want me to move out of state to a sober house, along with giving up my apartment. This is what they considered going to any length to get sober. I am pretty sure that this was just my after care plan. Because of all the other previous treatments and other institutions, this was the best thing for me. They told me that if my treatment and sobriety was that important to me then I should be willing to go to any length for it. They also suggested that maybe my daughter would be better off in foster care.

They stated that since I could not stay clean and sober that I was being selfish by continually taking my daughter through all of this. I knew within my heart that their after care plan for me was not going to happen, selfish or not. There was no way I was going to voluntarily put my child in child protection service, with my record I would never get her back. It made no sense to give up my apartment to go to an after care halfway house out of state for 90 days. Because once that 90 days was over where the hell was I suppose to live after that. And on top of that how in the world would child protection services even consider giving me my child with me having no place to live. I was not willing to go to this length for my sobriety. And I am still not willing to go to that length today, and that was maybe five years ago.

I wish I could say that I believe they had my best interest at heart, however I don't. I believe they were caught up in the best treatment plan for my sobriety. They did not have my best interest involved when it came to life after sobriety. When you really think about it, this was a 21 day impatient program. You add 90 days on to that, you'll come up with me having 111 days sober. However, now that I am homeless, without my child. What the heck you think is about to happen? More than likely I will start using again. Only this time it would be a lot worse. With no home and no child I probably would end up back in prison. What good would it be to be sober and in prison.

Going to any length is not a way to stay sober. At least not for me, actually it's not for a lot of other people otherwise people would not relapse. I have cleaned out garbage dumpsters all in an effort to get clean while in treatment. I've stood with my legs spread apart and my hands behind my back while other recovering addicts called me all sorts of names in an effort to break me down. I have worn life jackets and worked all day cleaning things that were already clean in an effort to make me change my ways and my thinking. Some treatment centers ask you to change the way you think in an effort to keep you sober. None of these treatment centers have worked for me. And the reason why they did not work for me is simple they never dealt with the root of the problem.

Addictions are mental, physical, social and psychological but most of all addiction is a sin. Therefore it calls for the spirit to be healed. The spirit is a borrowed invisible force that gives us life. It is not ours and we do not understand it. It was not ours before we were born and it is not ours when we die. The spirit belongs to God himself and to repair it we need God. God is the only person that can give us the opportunity to be reborn. This addiction has controlled our lives like sin controls mankind. It is not in our power to rid ourselves of its grip. If man could rid us of our addictions we would have been sober long before now. As I told you addiction is a sin and we were born in sin. For some of us, like me; we need God in order to recover. Since I planned on committing suicide I have been in constant contact with God, through prayer, meditation, praise and fasting. I am reading and studying my bible everyday for help. This is what is required for me to recover.

Now I'm not saying that traditional treatment does not work for some people. Studies show that it does, it just has not worked for me and many others. I had a friend who was an addict that used drugs and alcohol. He was also a diabetic. His addiction along with his illness killed him. He would not stop shooting drugs in his veins. With him being diabetic as well he lost limb after limb through amputation. This did not defer him from using drugs, therefore he over dosed and died. I spoke with him on several occasions before his death and there was just no life left in him. Drugs had completely left him hopeless. He too had been to treatment after treatment. I too have a drug addiction (crack cocaine) and it is the most powerful thing I have ever had to deal with. It consumes every part of my being. We will get into that part of my suicide later, however I knew what he was going through.

I have been hospitalized over and over for my heart condition. Doctor after doctor has told me that if I don't stop smoking crack I was going to die from it. I have come home from the hospital for heart problems and went directly to the dope house, and used crack. This world of addiction is not a simple choice as some would have you believe. At first it is a choice, when you first experience with it. But shortly afterwards it becomes a disease. A disease is a sickness that needs medication. And in today's world they have not found that medication yet.

My little sister was killed by a drunk driver. This guy stopped maybe two blocks from the scene of the accident and was outside his car crying. When the police found him the first thing he said, was tell me I didn't kill anybody. Well he had, my little sister. My point being in our sickness of addiction we know that our addiction is killing us and we still have no power over it to stop. Our addictions

Life By Suicide

are so strong we have to murder them. This guy was truly sorry for what he did, however I will be willing to bet that he is still drinking. For one thing he skipped out on bail and went back to his native land so that lets me know he is not willing to take responsibility for his actions. In order to recover from any addiction you have to be willing to take responsibility. Also, since there was no responsibility taken he has to drink in order to deal with what he did. You see this guy had a conscious that's why he stopped. He also had a heart that's why he was crying. The problem is that he also had an addiction and that's why he ran.

I sometimes volunteer at a food shelf where I pass out food to the hungry. I watch people who are homeless come into the food shelf everyday for food. Ninety percent of the time they are drunk, they even come with their six packs of beer and bottles of liquor. Even though I am not to serve anybody intoxicated I do. I say to myself it not for the grace of God, there I go. It gets truly cold in the state of Minnesota and I watch these people rather drink and live outside than pay to live indoors. I watch them rather drink than eat. And just like me I watch them rather die than live. All of these people have been to treatment over and over again. Yet they have not found the happiness needed to get sober. Beneath all addictions there is hurt feelings and unhappiness. I watched someone just leaving a funeral with me, pull their car over to the side of the road to shoot heroin. This person could not find a vein in his arms, he then pulled his pants down and he could not find a vein in his legs. He then tried his neck, finally as I was telling him to please take me home. He told me to get out of the car for a minute. I got out the car for about five minutes. When I finally went back to the car he was shooting heroin in his penis. Time and time again people have failed when it comes to traditional treatment. I have given you example after example of people suffering from addiction after treatment.

This is why Life by Suicide is necessary. I have found it necessary to pretend that I am dead in an effort to recover from my addictions. For me and millions of others the emotional damage caused by addiction is unbearable. Furthermore, addiction goes well beyond addiction. It is embedded in our soul. Addiction has become a part of us. It is no longer something that we just do. It lives within us and our bodies crave it just as our bodies crave food and water. It is no longer a choice for many addicts. And we are not just talking about drugs and alcohol. We are also talking about food, gambling, sex, and all others. I will say this one more time before I put a new twist on Life by Suicide. Addiction is a sin, it is completely against God's will for us. If you don't believe in God or his word the Bible then maybe this book is not for you. Because the twist that I am about to put on you comes directly from the Bible. And it is the reason we need God to heal us, also it is the reason we need to be reborn.

In the Bible it talks about us living in the last days. Those are the days right before Jesus will return to earth to complete God's will. Jesus said that in the last days we would experience wars and rumors of wars. The most powerful and richest country on earth started a war against drugs twenty years ago. We also have a war against the way we eat in this country. Our desire for unhealthy food has caused so many deaths from heart disease to diabetes. We have so many teenagers overweight and at risk of all sorts of disease. The pestilence and diseases that Jesus was talking about include these things too.

Why do you think that regardless of what people do they can not quit. Pestilence defined in the dictionary is " a contagious or infectious epidemic disease that spreads quickly and is often fatal". Look at what drugs and the epidemic of overeating is doing to our society. Our young people are loosing their lives to these things. And when you add the fact that the Bible says that "we are not fighting a war against people made of flesh and blood, but against the evil rulers and authorities of the unseen world, against those mighty powers of darkness who rule this world, and against wicked spirits in the heavenly realms, (Ephesians 6;12). So you see that our struggle to win this war is totally dependent upon God's help. None of us can win without the help of God. Why? For one thing we can't even see what or who we are fighting. This war was going on long before man even knew what was happening. The Bible is fulfilling its prophecy and we are in the middle of it. That's why the Bible says "pray at all times and on every occasion in the power of the holy spirit". God knows that our fight is one of spirit creatures that are looking to kill us. They are looking to keep us from the love of God. God knows in order for us to survive this war we will need his holy spirit. This

Life By Suicide

wicked ruler of this system of things is the same one who deceived Eve in the Garden of Eden. Yes! Satan is still our number one enemy and hater of God's will.

When it comes to drugs I tell you it seems as if Satan made them himself. Then he delivered them to earth. Never before has something devastated mankind the way drugs have in such a short period of time. Drugs have crossed age limits, race barriers, economic status, and religious beliefs. There is no limit to which drugs can not reach. Along with drug use there is crime, unsafe sex, disobedience to parents, lovers of money, hater's of what is right, sin just rampant everywhere. People with no morals, murder and hate, you name it and drugs are more than likely behind it. Yes! When Jesus mentioned the things that would happen in the last days he also meant addictions. If you really think about it what better way to get people away from God and his will for us? If someone is your enemy and hate you they are going to lie on you and do everything possible to turn your friends away from you.

The way out for those who believe is through Jesus Christ. There is no other name under heaven that can save mankind from this destruction. And when you believe things will change more than likely they will. I spoke to you earlier in this book about the happiest times in my life was while I was in prison. The reason for that is simple, the way that I felt about myself and the way that I was living when I was on the streets. For me, being arrested was like being rescued. My life on the outside was completely out of control. I love God regardless of all the troubles within me and when I am not in harmony with God my life is a wreck. Whenever I'm in jail or prison my total focus is on God and nothing else matters. I am able to pray and read my bible all day. I do a lot of fasting and praising God.

However the moment that I am released all that goes out the window sooner than later. Right now I am in prison mode and even though I am at home my mind is in a different mode. I need to be in this mode in order for me to die to myself. I know God is with me, because he has revealed to me things that should go into this book.

Once I was in prison and had been there for about a year. At the time I had decided to read the bible from beginning to end. Praying and fasting all along while reading and studying the Bible. Writing down scriptures and remembering them by heart. Studying what I had remembered, asking God for his wisdom and his will for me. I literally prayed twenty times a day and on some days more. The thing about prison you have nothing but time. It came to a point that I had formed another me. I had read and studied so hard and for so long that there were two of me. What I mean is that through all of my work my soul or spirit had been awaken. And it was now reading to me without me reading . When I was asleep my spirit was reading and praying for me. It was like someone else was inside of me. You can say that my subconscious mind was feeding back to me everything I was learning. It was repeating to me over and over the things within my spirit. I learned while in prison that it is truly possible to pray without ceasing. It is actually possible to pray always and never stop. If a person stand fast to God's word.

The Bible says in so many places to always pray. The Bible says in 1 Thessalonians 5; 16 -18 always be joyful! Keep on praying. No matter what happens always be thankful for this is God's will for you who belong to Christ Jesus". While in prison I lived in complete peace regardless of what was happening around me. The hate, the crimes, the homosexuality, the killings, there was nothing in me that was in prison. The only part of me that was incarcerated was my body and it didn't even know that it was there. I wasn't picked on, I had no enemies, and the prison guards had respect for me along with the inmates. I was truly free to move about as though I wasn't there. I respected everybody and everybody respected me. Of, course I followed the prison rules, that is a must for anybody to survive. I minded my own business and let people do as they saw fit. When the opportunity presented itself I would talk to anyone that wanted to hear about the Bible. Imagine being happy and at peace with ones self while in prison. There was nothing I wanted for or nothing I needed. I had never been closer to God in my entire life, not before then or after then. It is my hope and prayer that Life by Suicide will renew that relationship.

This is what I am after, to be in the arms of God Almighty. I have never been able to accomplish this while on the streets. It seems that the world and all of its desires engulfed me into its world of loose living. The sex and drugs, the money and the things that my sinful flesh wants to do. There is no glorification in drugs, however there are things about drugs that keep you interested and coming back. This is another reason drugs are so hard to get off of. Satan, when making drugs made it very appealing to the human soul. He made it to be desired for all times, once you were fool enough to use it. You would be trapped in a dark world of shame and you loose yourself in Satan's world and his demons. They are always around to keep you doing what is wrong in God's eye sight. They worked hard to make sure your desire remains around drugs.

    Listen, this is one of the reasons I had to pretend that I was dead. I have tried to leave my old friends along so that I can get clean off of drugs. I have told them not to come to my home with drugs and alcohol. They would come anyway. Sometimes I would be strong enough to tell them no, but more than likely I would fall short and end up using with them. Drugs would be no where on my mind and all of a sudden out of nowhere some one would knock on my door or call me on the telephone to use drugs. I have been cleaning my home and found drugs that should have not been there. This is what the bible meant when it said this fight is not one of human flesh and blood, but one of the rulers of this world and his demons in a heavenly realm. I have gotten dressed for church and waiting on my ride to go. Satan would send some one to my house with drugs and I never got to church. He puts all sorts of blocks in our paths so that we will fall short of God's love for us. Satan will not stop from trying to get us to leave God's grace. He will do anything at anytime and will use anybody to stop us.

    However we have a way out through Christ Jesus, he said through God's word, resist the devil and he will flee from you, draw close to God, and God will draw close to you". So we have an opportunity and the word and works of our lord to keep Satan and his demons from harming us. So once again get rid of all the filth and evil in your lives, and humbly accept the message God has planted in your hearts, for it is strong enough to save your souls. Since I have pretended to be dead I have not had one person come to my home to use drugs. As I told you earlier there is no reason for these people to come by. Even though all of these people claimed how much they cared for my daughter. Not one of them has come to check on her, they have not even called. My daughter left the message that she was going to finish school here in Minneapolis. And that her aunt, my sister was living here with her until the school year was over. That's why I told you earlier that these people were drug friends and nothing more. Therefore it didn't bother me to let them believe that I was dead.

You might be saying to yourself that I have used the Bible so many times throughout this book and talking about God. How could I make up a lie like that and expect God to bless me. Let me explain something to you, I am a human being that does not want to die. I am trying to save my life. When afraid of death a human will do whatever it takes to continue to live. I will not take the Bible and use it for my own selfish way. Have you not read in the Bible that when Abraham moved south with his wife Sarah. He told her to tell the people there that she was his sister because she was so beautiful. And Abraham did not want the men of the city to kill him so that they could take Sarah for a wife. And just as Abraham thought King Abimelech took his wife for himself. But God would not let the king touch Sarah. God went to king Abimelech in a dream and told him you are a dead man if you touch this woman for she is married, read Genesis chapter 20; 1-6.

Look I'm trying to save my life and if I believe that I have to let people think that I am dead, so be it. That does not take away from the truth and message in this book. We all must stand before Christ to be judge. We will each receive whatever we deserve for the good or evil we have done in these bodies, 2 Corinthians 5; 10. So what is between God and me is none of your business. It is as Jesus told Peter about the disciple whom he loved, when Peter asked what about him. Jesus said to Peter and I quote" if I want him to remain alive until I return, what is that to you. You follow me, John 21; 20-23". Basically Jesus was telling Peter to mind your own business. What is between me and him is none of your business. The things that I am telling and sharing with you are my own private personal experiences. These are things that I have lived the good and the bad. If I can put my personal life on paper to help others with the same problems that I have, then thank God.

When I decided to commit suicide, in order to save my life; it was not in the plan to write it in a book. However, I have had a book

Life By Suicide

of my life in me for many years. It is just now that I have come full circle to be able and discipline enough to do it. Once again God has sustained me. It has taken me only a few months to put it all down on paper. However, it has been fifty years living it. And I thank God for the time he has given me to get my life together. Without God I could do nothing. I feel thankful for all that God has done for me. I should not even be alive all the wrong I have participated in. The drugs I've used were enough to kill me alone. When I think of some of the things God has done for me, I feel like a fool for not serving God sooner.

I remember when I was living in Seattle. I was being evicted from my apartment because my daughter's mother had put a restraining order out on me for domestic violence. We had already been to court for custody of my daughter, in which I had temporary custody. We were trying to make our relationship work, but it wasn't. And she called the police on me, they told me not to come back to that apartment or else I would be going to jail. That would mean I would loose custody of my child. That night I prayed and the next morning extremely hard as I told God about my problems and my situation. I told him I had nowhere to take my child once I got off from work and picked her up from daycare. I asked God if he could please not only help me; but also that I needed a miracle. I had no idea what I was going to do. That following morning I dropped my child off at daycare and was headed downtown to catch the city bus to work. I had a lay over downtown while I waited for my next bus. So I decided to go into McDonald's and get a cup of coffee. While drinking my coffee standing looking out the window a man came over to me and asked me how I was doing. This guy looked like he was homeless and was not dressed as cleanly as someone should be.

I told him that I had a lot on my mind and I didn't have any money to give him. He continued to talk to me. I then told him to get out of my face and leave me alone. What he said to me next shocked me. His exact words were "I am not in your face and I am that miracle you prayed for this morning". I said to him, what did you say to me? He then said that I am that miracle you prayed for this morning. I talked to him about my situation he gave me his address and phone number. When I got off from work I called him. My daughter and I lived with him for six months.

Some people might not believe some of the interventions I've had in my life. And there is nothing I can do about that. I can only be honest and tell you what I lived and know. My life I lived and I know these things to be true. Rather or not someone else believe them is totally up to that person. I have come to the conclusion that God loves me and has shown me special kindness. I have done nothing to deserve this kindness and have no idea why God saw fit to give it to me. No! I take that part back when I said I have no idea. God wants me to be a testimony to his greatness. God is love, and he is forgiving along with being fair and showing true justice.

I've talked about a lot of bad that I have done, but have not said anything about some of the good I have done. This is because if you help somebody that has helped you, what good have you really done. If you only love the people that love you who have you loved. And seeing that I have done nothing to deserve God's loving kindness what can I boast about. All the people that I helped it was because God helped me help them and he alone deserves the entire glorification.

There is only one thing that I can say without boasting or bragging is that God has blessed me with the gift of prayer. I have always known how to pray and mostly all of my prayers are answered. I believe that God has blessed us all with some kind of gift or special talent. It is up to us to use what we have been given. Some of us don't believe God exist today as he did in Bible times. The thing that bothers me about this kind of thinking is how can you call yourself a Christian when you don't believe the prophets and the followers of Jesus Christ. The word Christian means Christ like. If God is the same as he always was and is, how is this thinking possible?

I believe that God does not make mistakes and that his word can not return to him untrue. Therefore when his prophets of old talked about the coming of Jesus Christ those things they foretold were true and have become true. When God placed the moon and sun in the sky or heavens that was because that's where he wanted them. He wanted them there in Bible times and they are still there today. When God placed man on the earth that is where he wanted them and they are still here today. How we die and end up in heaven I have no idea. When we were perfect and had not sinned yet God did not want us in heaven. What makes people think that he wants us in heaven after all we have done by disobeying him and all the wickedness we have participated in. When God sent angels to help and protect his people then, he still does it today. The Bible says angels are servants sent from God to care for those who will receive salvation, (Hebrews 1; 14). God is the same today as he was yesterday. God forgave men then and he forgives men today. God answered prayers then and he answers prayers today. God loved us then and he loves us today. God protected man then and God protects man today. God punished men then and God punishes men today. God clothed the lilies of the field then and God clothes the lilies of the field today. God hated sin then and God hates sin today. God hated homosexuality then and God hates homosexuality today. God did not like murder then and God does not like murder today. God did not like people serving other God's then and God does not like people serving other God's today.

Now there are some things that God allowed then that he does not approve of today. We no longer need to sacrifice animals to repent and receive forgiveness. God sent his son Jesus to die for our sins therefore we no longer have to do that. We can go directly to God through Jesus Christ now. God allowed men in the beginning to be sexually involved with their family members to populate the earth. The earth is already populated now so that is no longer allowed. These things were done to fulfill God's plan. And while no one can understand God he has made it possible for us to understand his will for us.

Holy, Holy, Holy is the Lord God Almighty, The One Who Always Was, Who Is, And Who Is Still to Come!

Hopefully you now have some kind of understanding about God's existence. For God is forever and will never change. All praises and glory belongs to Jehovah God Almighty.

CHAPTER THREE
The Devil's Drug

There is more dying I must do in order for me to completely commit suicide. The Bible uses the phrase, deaden or put to death. Actually the Bible says deaden in one version of the Bible. And in another version of the Bible it says put to death. So the scripture reads "so put to death the sinful, earthly things lurking within you. Have nothing to do with sexual sin, impurity, lust, and shameful desires. Don't be greedy for the good things of this life, for that is idolatry" (Colossians 3;5).

One of the other things I must put to death is my drug addiction. It is lurking inside of me looking to destroy me and keep me separated from God. I chose not to talk about my drug addiction to much when I was speaking about my alcoholism. Because, to me; they are two different addictions. While both are mind altering drugs, alcohol has never done to me the things that crack cocaine has done. I can truly say that I have never dreamed about alcohol, whereas I have had so many dreams about crack cocaine. I have never robbed anyone for alcohol, I have for cocaine. There has never been a time when I was not drinking that I smelled alcohol. I have literally smelled and tasted cocaine when I was not even thinking about it or using it. The effect that crack cocaine has had on my life physically and mentally is devastating. And the psychological effect is even worse.

This part of me must be murdered at all cost. The first time I ever used this drug it was over for me. I was completely hooked with the first hit. Crack cocaine had taken complete control over my life the very first moment I was introduced to it. The terrible thing about this is, I was leaving from an Alcohol Anonymous meeting after receiving my one year clean and sober medallion. I was proud of myself for being clean and sober for a full year. A drug dealer I knew from the neighborhood seen me walking and gave me a ride home. Now my idea of celebrating one year sober was to have a drink. Even this drug dealer knew that didn't make any sense. He told me that if you have been sober for one year why have a drink now. I told him that after a year; one drink would not hurt me. Boy, was I wrong! Anyway we stopped at the liquor store and got something to drink. He came over to my home and had a few drinks with me. He then asked me if I mind if he bagged up his drugs and that he would pay me. I told him to go ahead that it would not bother me. The more I drank the better I felt. After a while I asked him what using crack was like, because he was a smoker as well as a dealer. He smoked some and let me try it as well. That was the biggest mistake in my life. And from that moment on I have been hooked on crack cocaine.

Like I said earlier the amount of times that I have been to treatment was not only for alcohol but mostly for cocaine. My prison time was once for alcohol, but the other two times was for crack cocaine. I immediately started spending every dime on cocaine. I was spending my paycheck from work before I even got paid. I was bouncing checks and stealing to support this habit. I begin to commit arm robberies and clip people for their wallets. This drug would not allow me to stop. Ten dollars of crack was not enough and one thousand dollars was not enough. I would use crack all day and all night. I would be up for days without food and very little water, just smoking crack. It got to a point that I was willing to do almost anything for this drug.

I remember jumping off a third floor balcony in order to keep my drugs from the police. The police raided a drug house as I was buying drugs. Instead of throwing my drugs on the floor I ran to the back of the house and jumped off the balcony as police were kicking down the door. When, I landed I broke my ankle in two different places. On a broken ankle I walked or crawled four blocks to my home. I then continued to smoke crack for three days calling the drug dealers to me. By the time I went to the hospital my ankle had swollen so large it was the size of a cantaloupe. As if that was not bad enough I later cut off my cast after about two weeks while smoking crack cocaine. And my ankle has never healed properly until this day. The reason I cut my cast off is because it had gotten wet and was itching. I had made about five trips in the pouring down rain to get more drugs. Alcohol had never done anything like this to me before. My life was really out of control now and it seemed I could do nothing about it. This was another blow to me personally separating myself from God. I knew I was me, but I was no longer me. Crack cocaine had engulfed my soul it had literally become entangled with my spirit. And more of the God in me was lost. My separation with God had gotten larger than ever before. It was Michael against Michael, it was mind against body, it was spirit against soul, it was life against death, and crack against the crack in me. This drug would call for you or at least it did me.

Once it was in my bloodstream from the very first time I used it, it slowly became me. I could not stop thinking about it nor could I stop wanting it. This drug is so powerful I swear that Satan the devil designed it, manufactured it and delivered it to earth himself. There is no way that a human being could have invented this drug to do what it does. This is way above our heads and understanding. This was done by a spiritual being with the power to completely destroy ones being. And only one person, only one spiritual being has been trying to destroy mankind from the beginning and that, is Satan the Devil. He was the one that came to Eve as a serpent and lied.

The damage he caused then still lives with us today. What he wanted was to separate us from God. He later went to Job and tried to separate Job from God. I'm pretty sure you know that story. And is he not the same being that tried to convince our lord Jesus Christ to sin against God. I, tell you he alone created crack cocaine. This is another example that this war that we are fighting is not just against flesh and blood. We are fighting against wicked spirits in heavenly places. This is why we need the protection of God. We alone can not stand up to these spirit creatures because we can't even see them.

That is why I must rely on God. I can't even remember the amount of times I've tried to get off of this drug. I would work forty hours per week only to spend every penny in four hours on crack. I remember using so much crack cocaine that my heart was beating so fast and so hard. I knew if I took another hit my heart would burst. I took a hit anyway. I can also recall using so much that I was hearing and seeing things that were not there. This is when my suicidal thoughts started. I wanted this drug out of my life and the only way I felt I could get rid of it was to commit suicide.

I never thought about killing myself when using alcohol. My guilt and depression was so heavy and often that I could not bear me any longer. I committed a robbery for drugs and got caught. I went to prison and I was happy because I felt like at least I have a chance now to get sober. When I was released from prison all that morning I was afraid and nervous. I knew that this drug was outside waiting for me. I did not want to leave prison. I was correct my addiction to crack cocaine was waiting for me and I was back to using the same day I was released. Within 90 days I was back in jail for more arm robberies and once again I was glad. The judge that sentenced me appeared to be very wise in his job. Or he was touched by God in my behalf. Because he only sentenced me to the minimal amount of jail time allowed under the law.

However, I will never forget what he said to me. He told me Mr. Clark you are either a damn fool or you have a serious drug problem and you need help. I believe that you need help and that's why I refuse to give you so much jail time. But I am not letting you off the hook that easy. I am sending you to a one year impatient treatment center, also you can not be released to the streets or a half way house. You are to go directly from prison into treatment.

Therefore Mr. Clark that means that if your prison sentence is over and there is no bed available, then you will remain in prison until there is one available. Do you understand that Mr. Clark. I said yes sir with a large smile on my face. I even thank him over and over because now I definitely had a chance. This is how I ended up in the one year drug treatment center I talked about earlier. I did stay in prison longer than I was suppose too, but that was fine with me. I do not want to over lap with my writing but this is also during the time I met Pat and Teresa. At this point I was feeling good about myself and life again. I had been sober for over 16 months and even though it was in prison I was cool.

Now with one year in a safe place like treatment I was really beginning to feel great. My thinking is that I am home at last. I was feeling free of my drug and alcohol addictions and my life was beginning to make sense again. If you have never been addicted to anything then it might be difficult to understand how hope feels good. Most people take hope for granted, however to the addict hope is not so easily obtained.

Hope is like breathing fresh air to an addict. Hope is no longer an invisible suggestion of your imagination. Hope becomes an emotion to the recovering addict. Hope becomes a weapon to help the addict fight off the fear of using again. All addicts live with fear constantly, rather it be the fear of using drugs again or gambling or eating. Whatever the addict is addicted to the fear of doing that again is always there. We as addicts are afraid of becoming useless again. Hope is the only powerful tool we have to make us feel better about ourselves.

And when we relapse that hope disappears and we find ourselves right back where we started. Feeling defeated all over again, the depression returns, hope seems to have gotten away from us and there we go into that dark alley of hopelessness. Because the man in the mirror has returned and our image of ourselves gets worse than it was before. We go right back to the one and only thing that allows us to escape ourselves, which is our addiction. We live in this dark world until we gather the strength to try again. For some it takes days, but for many others it can take months and for the drug addict it can even take years. The reason it take us so long to recover from relapse is because we are fighting ourselves. If you are in a fight with yourself you can't win. This process keeps us from wanting to face ourselves because it's hard to face you when you don't like you. Therefore the addict lives two different lives. One life is of fear and the other life is of hopelessness. We become our biggest enemy and our fight continues. We believe that there is no way out for us because we have been through this process over and over. We are tired and believe that there is no reason to keep putting ourselves through this never ending roller coaster. We believe, just to fail, and we fail when we believe. And what happens is that we come to the conclusion that there is no hope for us. Whatever we think and believe it just does not turn out the way we thought or hoped for.

This is where killing ourselves comes into the picture. I don't believe there is any addict that has been through this cycle that has not thought suicide before. If you are an addict with a serious addiction and you have been going through this for years and have been defeated over and over again suicide has crossed your mind.

You may have not acted on the thought, but you know for yourself that it has been thought about. It is literally impossible to live in a world of self defeating behavior and not think about ending your pain and suffering. I have thought about it thousands of times and acted on it once. My suicide by cop attempt was just that. It was an attempt to end the pain and suffering in my life. The cycle of my addiction had seemed to given me no other reasonable alternative except suicide. Thank God almighty that it did not turn out the way I had planned and hoped for. I now have come full circle and understand that there is a way out of my addictions and the world of thought that keeps me in it. I now understand that I have the power to change the way I live my life. I now understand that addiction is me not loving myself. For if I loved myself; I would not do any of the things that I do to defeat me.

The solution is to kill everything inside of me that makes me dislike me. This is why Life by Suicide is the most important thing that we can do for ourselves. Those painful and suffering things that we have allowed to live inside our lives must be put to death. It is not enough to just talk about these things with a therapist, no; it's time to commit murder of ourselves. Our talking days are over we need death in our lives so that we can live. We can no longer allow sin to rule our lives. If you can remember back when you were a child and had not done any wrong in your life, you will see a happy worry free person.

If you continue to look you will find the first thing that personally separated you from God. I'm not talking about your first spanking or your first state of sadness. You could have been sad because; you did not get what you wanted for Christmas. I'm talking about the first time you knew that your spirit had been attacked. Rather you did it to yourself or some one did it to you. I'm talking about that thing that changed your way of life. And the way you thought about life. This is the point you will find the beginning of your own pain and suffering.

And it is at this point that life turned on you. No matter how small or large this incident was it caused your thinking to change and you began to look for a way out.

For some of us it might be the lost of a parent at such an early age. For others it might be alcohol and for others it might be rape or being sexually abused. It could even be being teased as a child. The size of your discomfort does not matter. What matters is this is the point where you started to dislike yourself and began to look for a new you. And what we found was our DNA; sin itself, thanks to Adam.

Once we found our sinful selves our nature guided us to the negative symptoms of our lives. We therefore built upon that like we were building a house. But we never found the right tools to complete the house we were trying to build. Therefore our pain and suffering grew larger and larger. Let me see how I can put this so that you will truly understand what I am talking about. Have you ever been asleep and someone woke you up for no apparent reason that was important to you. And the moment you woke up you found yourself angry, because your sleep had been interrupted. Now you are finding it hard to function in a peaceful state of mind. I mean little things are making you upset. This is what I meant by finding that sinful DNA. Once it's awoken it takes on a life of its own and seeks out something or someone to comfort it. Being woke up out of your sleep you won't find that comfort until you go back to sleep giving your body the rest that it needed before you were awaken.

For the sin in our lives we need to go back to God for the comfort we need to rid ourselves of that negative DNA. Because God created us and he knows the amount of hair on our heads, he alone can cure us. The bible says" trust in the lord with all your heart; do not depend on your own understanding. Seek his will in all you do, and he will direct your paths" Proverbs 3; 5. God is the only alternative we have. Who else can deliver us from the pain and suffering from our sinful self? Psalm 32; 5 say "finally, I confessed all my sins to you and stopped trying to hide them. I said to myself, I will confess my rebellion to the lord. And, you forgave me! All my guilt is gone". With all of our guilt gone we can look at ourselves with new eyes and a new heart. We begin to like ourselves again. We begin to realize that God is our only hope for salvation from ourselves. And with this new found suicide we can begin to live.

We have finally found our baby like self, who we use to be. That all so good innocence. For, that is the state in which we were born. We were able to love with no reason or hidden agenda. We had laughter in our hearts and joy in our souls. Life to us was peaceful and without worry. Because God loved us at that time and yet we knew nothing of him. His gift to us was free. You see that our DNA also is of God. He formed us in his own image and therefore we can return to life as God meant for it to be.

Now that we have recognized that God is our only way out we can confessed to God our wicked ways and be forgiven. We have committed suicide and our old self is dead. However we must kill all of our old sickness. Therefore I must continue to confess to God the rest of my crack cocaine addiction and all the wrong I did to supply myself.

One of the greatest sins I believe I have ever committed in my life was receiving money from my Bible studies and using that money for drugs. My soul was so damaged and my mind just ate at my bones to the point I couldn't even think of God. I knew I had committed a sin that leads directly to death. I remember trying to pray to God for his forgiveness and could not even lift or bow my head to pray. My mind would not even consider the thought of prayer. Until this day I know that this is the worse sin I have ever committed. I have never felt so terrible in my life. And regardless that all sin is sin to God some sin is worse than others. Nothing I had ever done from robberies to whatever. Had the effect on my mind and spirit that using God's people to use drugs did. My complete spirit was devastated and my mind would not give me comfort.

All that I could think of was when in the Bible a man and his wife lied about a certain amount of money that they were going to give to the church. In the process they changed their minds and lied about it. Actually this is exactly what the Bible says about it. I am going to write word for word how the Bible explains it.

Then Peter said, Ananias, why has Satan filled your heart? You lied to the Holy Spirit, and you kept some of the money for yourself. The property was yours to sell or not sell, as you wished. And after selling it, the money was yours to give away. How could you do a thing like this? You weren't lying to us but to God. As soon as Ananias heard these words, he fell down to the floor and died. And it goes on to say that about three hours later his wife came in. She was asked by Peter the price of the land they had sold and not knowing what had happened to her husband, she lied. And Peter said to her, how could the two of you even think of doing a thing like this, conspiring together to test the spirit of the lord. Just outside that door are the men that buried your husband, and now they will carry you out too. Instantly she fell to the floor and died". You can read this story for yourself in the book of Acts chapter 5 verses 3-10.

When I lied to my Bible studies and I say studies because it happened more than one time in my life. I was to use that money for food, at least that's the lie I used to get it. When I turned around and used it for drugs, man was I afraid when the drugs wore off and it really hit me what I had done. To me this was the greatest sin I had committed in my entire life. Fortunately, God has allowed me to live. And once again almighty God had shown me his kindness and mercy. When Jesus said sin no more or something worse might happen to you. That is a sin I will never commit again. I have never been so afraid in my life. And I have had guns put to the back of my head before with someone threatening to kill me. Even writing about this incident scares me.

Praise God for his kindness towards me. I have done nothing to deserve the amount of love and favor God has shown me. But I do know that I to will be punished and stand before God for the good and bad that I have done. None of us has the power to prevent the day of our death. There is no escaping that obligation, that dark battle. I just pray that at my time of death I am doing God's will and not mine.

My addiction to crack cocaine caused me to use the people of God for my own purpose. It was not my intentions from the beginning because I really did need food for my daughter and me. However as soon as my Bible study left, my mind automatically changed from the happiness of having money for food, to the use of drugs. That is one of the powerful things about this drug. It literally takes on a life of it's own without a person being focused on it. It's almost ironic that at this point in my book we are on this subject. Allow me to give you a perfect example of what I'm talking about. It has been well over a month since I even thought seriously about drugs. Being an addict it definitely has crossed my mind however I have so far been able to ignore those thoughts. I at no point have a desire with the normal passion of the past.

Yesterday I received a lump sum of money that I was not expecting any time soon. Immediately my mind began to wonder on drugs and the sex that goes along with the high of using drugs. The choices of young ladies that I thought about calling came to mind without even thinking about it. The scent of the drug came to reality as if I was using right then. The thought of going to the store to get the drug pipe I would need came along with all these other thoughts. My mind forgot all about my writing and the need to commit suicide through confessing my sins to God all vanished in an instant. I knew at that very point it was time for some serious praying. I immediately got up and got on my hands and knees and prayed to God about my problem.

Previously I had come to the conclusion that I would have to cut my death short. That is people believing that I was dead. The reason I needed to cut short my death was based on business that needed to be attended to. Also before I made the decision to pretend to play dead I had an appointment for some minor surgery. And although I called my doctor to see if I could put it off. She was concerned and advised me of the need to have these test done as soon as possible. This unexpected money which kicked in my addiction used this for the reason to get me to go outside and feed it. However like I said I prayed about this to God. I asked God to take away these thoughts and feelings and to give me guidance as to what I should do.

My daughter was also concerned, because she said daddy you aren't going anywhere are you. She has lived with me through my many years of addiction and knew exactly what was going on in my mind. Anyway I prayed throughout the day and here I am writing the very next day, no drugs or alcohol at all. My praying got me through yesterday and it will get me through today. The thoughts and feelings I had when I received that money has left my mind, praise God. Never before for as long as I can remember when it

Life By Suicide

came to that amount of money did I fight off my addiction with such power and force.

Not only did God answer my prayers but I had a dream last night telling me it was not safe for me to go outside because God had not finish healing me. As soon as this dream was over I jumped up out of bed and thanked God through prayer. Because I knew that God was watching over me. Therefore once again I give thanks and all praise to God almighty. For he alone deserves worship. This dream renewed my strength and gave me the will power to carry on with my book which I believe is God's work for me. Without God I would be using drugs right now. I am so happy that my lord loves me regardless of all the wicked and evil things that I have done. I am so happy that God forgives and remember my sins no longer. Unlike mankind who say they forgive you and then say but I can't forget it. God is good. This is what I've been telling you all this time about committing suicide so that you can live. We need to get rid of all, things that cause us to live a wicked life. Just by handing everything over to God and confessing our sins, he will help us. "Are any of you suffering you should keep on praying about it, (James 5; 13).

It is so important that you pray about everything that cause you harm, no matter what". Look at it this way in order to form a good relationship with anyone you have to communicate with that person. You have to get to know that person, and furthermore you have to spend time with that person. This is the only way to become friends. It is the same way with God we have to spend time with him, through our prayers. We have to get to know him through reading and studying his word the bible. This way we form a relationship with God and we become friends.

Can you imagine being friends with the creator of everything? Would you not want to be friends with someone who has the power to answer prayers? Would you not want to be friends with someone who would forgive you and never bring it up again? Would you not want to be friends with the only person that can grant life or death? Well, you can all you need to do is form a relationship with God and he will draw close to you. What a great gift our lord has given us and it was given to us freely at no cost to us. God defends all who comes to him for protection. And I thank God for his protection.

My addiction has taken me places I would have never gone as the example above, about the Bible study money. I can't write down all the things I did trying to get drug money, but I will try and be honest. That is the purpose of this book when it all boils down to it. Nowhere in this book is it meant to glorify drugs or the use of drugs. There is no glory in the use of drugs. There is nothing there except the taking of ones soul. My addiction has never brought me joy or happiness. It has only brought temporary relief from a troubled person. And once the drug wore off the troubled person was still there, only to be more troubled. This book is also not designed to boast about the drugs in my life. My drug use has brought me nothing but shame and left me nothing to be proud of. The Bible talks about someone; who boast about how much they can drink. And in my case I will just add drugs to the meaning of this verse. Isaiah 5; 22 says "destruction is certain for those who are heroes when it comes to drinking, who boast about all the liquor they can hold". The Bible also says that liquor is for the dying and wine is for the deeply depressed (proverbs 31; 6).

One of the things that my addiction has done for me is caused my health to fail and that is nothing to glorify or boast about. However, after Life by Suicide my life to alcohol and drugs will be over. My life belongs to God and his will is all that I want to do with the rest of my life. I know that my story deserves to be told in hopes and prayers that it might help others. With God's blessing it will do just that. May God bless the words of this book! I have never trusted myself when it comes to my addiction because I have always failed to conquer it. But this time with the complete help of God it will not be a problem. I do want to say that I will have to find other resources to keep me aware of my addiction. It would be foolish of me and anyone else to believe that there won't be any temptations and trails. I must remember my addiction is what they call cunning, baffling and powerful. It will with the help of the wicked one himself, Satan try and attack me when I least expect it.

Also I must understand that I will need to replace everyone I know and everyplace I go. I can no longer be around people who drink and use drugs. And as I said in the very beginning of my book those are the only people I know. Knowing that I have to fight this fight against Satan and his demons, I will need all the help I can get. Even though once you kill something it is dead and have no more life, we have to remember that we are not dead. And this addiction has lived with us for so long it is in our DNA. Plus, Satan will not let us off that easily. If our lord Jesus Christ was tested by the evil one, you had better believe he is waiting for us. Please understand that Satan is no match for our God therefore we need to keep him close by. It is not enough for us to just believe in God we also need to practice it in our deeds.

In the Bible book of James chapter 2 verse 19 it says "do you still think it's enough just to believe that there is one God? Well, even the demons believe this and they tremble in terror. Fool! When will you ever learn that faith that does not result in good deeds is useless"? I therefore as well as you, since we are trying to recover from our addictions need to practice good deeds. We are going to need something different in our lives. One of those things for me will be to watch what I do and not sin by what I say. I will stay away from my old friends and life style. Because, I have had enough of the evil things in my past! All the wild parties, and the immorality, and the lust, all of my drunkenness and drug use. The lying to myself and others, I have had enough of living in hopelessness. I have had enough of not being happy. It is my turn to live the life God intended for me to live. I already know that once I show my face from being dead all of my old friends will come by if for no other reason but to be nosy. To find out what happened. And this will be my first set of test and trails. This will be my opportunity to tell them in a firm but respectable manner not to come to my home anymore. That I am doing Gods will for me and that I no longer use drugs or alcohol. The reason I said in a respectable manner because God is a God of peace and if I am doing his will I must first try peaceful ways. If they continue to come by then I will have to show my dislike for their actions. That will call for aggressive behavior and not violent behavior.

Four weeks have gone past since I last wrote on this book because it has taken that long for me to get back to my new self.

While I fought off my temptations to use drugs and alcohol I once again failed. One moment I was strong and confident in my new found ability to conquer these addictions and I failed again. It seemed to me all of my beliefs and writing was for nothing. Once again I allowed my weak soul to fall into the hands of the wicked one and his demons. I was afraid to bow my head in prayer to God and ask for his forgiveness. It was extremely hard for me to focus on anything but my failure and my worthlessness. I once again felt hopelessness and began to believe that I was nothing more than a complete failure.

I said to myself that you have been writing about killing your old self and becoming a new man in order for you to live. And as soon as you got a little money there you went. I was so down on myself and was unable to pray that two weeks had gone by. My only thoughts were how can you help anybody else and you can't even help yourself? Who do you think wants to believe the writer if the writer failed to do what he is teaching? How can I even ask people to think about my philosophy if it didn't even work for me?

However I slowly came back to the real reason for Life by Suicide and realized that I had not yet died to myself. And neither had I completely confessed all of my sins because I had not yet finished this book and all that it requires from me. From that point on I began to look at the positive side of my relapse and realized that it to would be a part of this book. I at first struggled with adding my relapse as part of this book. However I came to the conclusion that without it my book would be no more than a lie.

This relapse is just as important as any other part of this book. When I realized that my mistake in using was also a learning process it became one of the most important things I needed to focus on. I realized that everybody makes mistakes and that we will probably make some more mistakes. But we also had not completely killed ourselves yet. My relapse has made me even stronger than I was before. Because now I understand that it is going to take a complete all around focus and awareness of our unseen enemy, Satan.

I understand truly now that he is never far away from us just waiting for us to feel over confident. Before I relapse I prayed to almighty God for help and I received that help. Feeling good about God's protection I literally forgot that Satan was also watching me and waiting. And once I let my guards down he jumped on me like

Life By Suicide

white on rice. He was not far away from me and knew that God had given me his protection and I failed to follow it. My dream told me that I was not ready. And I paid great attention to that dream and remained in God's grace and protection. However two days later I felt more confident and didn't seek God's guidance in the matter. Mostly, I had not had any further dreams, and also because the money was burning a hole in my pockets. I forgot all about the evil one. My desire to be strong proved to be weak.

Drugs were not on my mind nor were they in my heart when I decided to end my physical appearance of death. I was only focused on paying some bills and shopping for things needed in the house. However, I was not as strong as I thought I was and neither was I ready. However at some point I would have to go outside and people who thought I was dead would eventually see me. My focus and intentions were true to my writings and beliefs. Failure was not anywhere in the picture. This is what makes this mistake or relapse so important because without it my strength would not have gotten any stronger.

This has allowed me to know that nothing can keep us from the love of God. Regardless of what we do, we can always return to God and ask for forgiveness and he will welcome us with open arms. As long as we come humbly knowing what we had done wrong and seeking to repent of our mistakes.

As I said earlier it was very hard for me to go back to God in prayer, because I felt so bad for what I had done. The one thing that kept me from falling so deep into my old way of depression was that I still had God in my heart. Even though I knew that I had disappointed God, I still knew that he was waiting for me to come to him and ask for his forgiveness. I knew that once I got over feeling bad I could go to him. And most of all I really didn't have to wait, we can always go to God for his help. I believe that it was my own guilt that stopped me from going to God any sooner. Also that is what Satan's job is, to keep us believing that God will not forgive us this time. And to keep us feeling so bad about ourselves that we won't seek out God.

I remember at one point in my life I was feeling so bad about myself and so loaded down with depression. I needed someone or something to uplift my spirits and to give me something to live for. My relationship with God at that time was not a friendship where as I felt comfortable seeking his love and help. Satan the devil had me believing that I had done too much wrong in my life for God to ever forgive me.

However, I was in spiritual pain and needed something to bring me out of my depression and low self esteem. So I decided while looking at a television commercial to call this physic on the commercial for help. Therefore I dialed the phone number listed on the television screen. Someone answered the phone and put me on hold, while music played in the back ground. Finally a human being picked up the telephone and thanked me for calling the physic hot line. They informed me that they would need to get some personal information about me before I would be able to talk with the physic. They asked me a lot of general questions, such as my age, birth place, job title and etc. This whole process took about 10 to 15 minutes and I was being charged $6.99 per minute.

Finally I was talking to the lady that claimed to be a physic. She tells me that I am going to live for a long time. And, that I was about to receive three or four thousand dollars within the next 30 days or so. She also tells me that I seemed to be depressed and that I also seem unhappy. She continues her evaluation of me with nothing more than general answers from questions asked by me that could apply to the average person. I guess this went on for about one hour when I finally told her that I was not happy with the service I was receiving from her. Because, all of your answers could fit anybody and furthermore I gave most of this information to the person that screened me before I ever talked with you. She lost her temper while apologizing to me about not liking the service and hung up the phone on me.

So about 30 days later I got a bill in the mail for almost $410.00, it was at this point I decided I was not going to pay this bill. I said to myself. Why would I pay this bill, when I received no hope and I was even more depressed after talking with her than I was before I first called? Therefore I called customer service and tried to make my complaint with them. They in turn told me that regardless of not receiving the answer that I wanted to hear, I still used the service and I needed to pay my bill. I told them that everything that she said to me could apply to anybody. And, furthermore she told me things that I told the person that screened me before I ever talked with her.

They said that no matter what; it was my bill. I then accused them of cheating people. They responded by asking me how did I want to pay by check or credit card. I told them I was not going to pay the bill. I was told they would send it to a collection agency for payment and that it would go against my credit score. I then told them that they could do whatever they felt they had to do, but if that woman was really a physic she would have known I was not going to pay this bill and I hung up. I have never heard from them or any collection agency since.

That story is the perfect example of why we need to only trust in God to help us with all of our problems. Not only did I not find any hope or happiness in my conversation with this so called physic. But I almost wasted over $400.00 on something that was not true or helpful. Did I receive three or four thousand dollars in the next 30 days or so! Yes, I did, however I already knew that because it was tax time and I had already filed my taxes. This was a great lesson for me that I realized so many years later. I am so glad today that I went through that relapse, because I know without any reasonable doubt that only God can guide me to true happiness and peace of mind, body and spirit. I knew this before but this served as a recent and personal reminder.

I have depended on my own wisdom and understanding and I think too much sometimes. My wisdom is foolish and can not guide me through life. I need to murder all within me in order to make room so that God can enter me and take control of my life.

Sometimes we need to move out the way and allow God's will to take place in our lives. The Bible says that we need to trust in the lord with all of our hearts; do not depend on our own understanding. It says for us to seek God's will in all that you do and he will direct your paths,(Proverbs 3;5). My life is getting better the more I write and study the bible. However, I still have a long way to go before I can honestly say that I now can live a good life because I have killed all wickedness within me. My effort to be reborn is a personal one, just as yours must be. It is up to everyone to go to God himself. No one can do this for us we are truly on our own when it comes to repentance.

I stopped my writings and went to a mental illness chemical dependency program. I, came to realize that I would not be able to stay clean and sober without first dealing with my mental illnesses. How did I find this out, I relapsed again. My heart was broken and I did not understand how such a thing could happen. My heart and my mind were both in the right place and I felt like I was sincere in all of my doings and thoughts. Therefore I said to myself something is not right with me. So therefore I decided to seek professional help with my problems and I checked into an impatience treatment center that dealt with both mental health and drug and alcohol addictions. While there I sometimes wondered what this would do to my concept of Life by Suicide. Only to find out that my concept was similar to the twelve step program that was offered there. I found out that I still had to kill off my old self. However, I first had to deal with my mental illness. And the only way for me to do that was to seek help from a mental health professional, a psychologist. I found out that I needed medication to stabilized and maintain reasonable thought process. I also needed help with the lack of energy and motivation due to my depression. I also was diagnosed with post traumatic stress disorder as well as agoraphobia.

My mental health would not allow me to stay clean and sober under any circumstances until it was brought under control. Therefore I struggled with Life by Suicide. My concept was not wrong it was my mental illness that caused my relapses. It is still a fact that a person must completely kill off their old selves in order to be reborn and find true happiness. While in treatment the previous seven times there were four things I was just not willing to do. One, I was not willing to work the 12 steps. I felt like I could maintain my sobriety without digging up old garbage. Two, I was not willing to get a sponsor; because I felt as if no other man could possibly tell me how to live my life and suggest to me what I needed to do based on their past experiences. Three, I was not willing to expose my dirty secrets to anyone. Why would I do that? That's the reason they are secrets. And four I refused to believe that I had to possibly go to meetings for the rest of my life. All of the four above things were not for me.

However, while in treatment I was praying to God about being there and asking him. Why do you answer all and any prayers of mine, and yet you are unwilling to answer my prayer about taking these addiction away from me? I was telling God; is this some kind of test for me or a mountain that I have to climb alone without your protection and guidance. I was asking God in my prayer why have you left me here alone and to please help me. You know how many tears I have shed over this addiction. You alone God have seen my depression and heart ache over my addictions. You alone know my heart and thoughts, what is the problem and why have you not helped me and given me the answer to my prayers. I have asked you with a heavy heart and tears running down my face not to let me live any longer. Please, Jehovah God, tell me what I am doing wrong.

Once I finished praying and even before I got off my hands and knees I was given the answer. I am not saying to you that I heard this voice like many times before in my life. But I am telling you that I had a revelation or a spiritual awakening. And in this awakening I was told, Michael, I have loved you for over fifty years and have always been there for you. Our relationship is also a partnership. I have done my part now do yours. I have loved you so much that I have sent you to treatment eight times and you still don't get it. One, work the steps, two get a sponsor, three go to meetings and you will stay clean and sober. And four don't question me like that again.

After this revelation or awakening things became very clear to me and my treatment was successful. I graduated with no reservations about what I had to do. My God had saved me again. All thanks and glory belongs to Jehovah God for my recovery and my life.

I came to realized and believe that the programs of these anonymous groups were put in place by God. God alone knew that some of his sheep and followers were going to need help because of their addictions of alcohol and drugs. He knew that we could never get to him if we did not clean our bodies and minds from our addictions. He knew that the evil one, Satan the devil would use all sorts of tricks and chemicals to keep people away from him. So once again God has given us a way out just as he did when he gave his only begotten son Jesus Christ to die for our sins.

I spoke earlier in my book about nothing can keep us from the love of God. And once again I invite you to read Romans, 8; 38-39 where the bible says "that I am convinced that nothing can keep us from the love of God. Not angels or demons" I just quoted some parts of these verses to you so please go back to your own Bible to see for yourself. These programs are God's doing and his alone. The thanks and praise for these programs belong to God and him alone. The reason that I said that is because some of us in these programs give to much honor and praise to two mere human beings, Bill and Bob. These men were no more than tools used by God to implement a program of recovery for God's purpose. They are not saints and even in the big book of Alcohol Anonymous, in the reading of how it works states that. I also realized while in treatment that what God has called and made clean let no man call it dirty. Earlier in my book I said that for some of us we need more than just a simple program of recovery. And that they just had not worked for us. And while some of us are truly sicker than others does not mean that these programs doesn't work. It just means that for some of us it will take longer to recover. It means that for some of us, we will need outside help, such as medication and etc.

I even understand a lot more about my relapse and how it tied into my recovery and my book. First of all I needed to learn that in order for me to continue with God's blessings of my book. I had to realize that God's hands and will is involved in these programs. And that I could not continue with Life by Suicide and at the same time disrespect a program that God himself made. I had to realize that Life by Suicide is a last minute call to all of the suffering addicts who have been to treatment over and over and are still suffering. Life by Suicide is just a tool used by the same God to call to him those of us that are sicker than others, like myself.

Today is Tuesday May 19, 2009 and from the moment I woke up on May 15, 2009 my addiction was in full bloom. It literally woke up with me. There were no major events that had taken place. I had no problems or stress at the time. I just woke up with this other person, which is my addictive side of Michael.

Understand that for the sicker than others addict, there is another person living inside of us. That other person is the addict that has grown with us for years. It has a life of it's own inside our bodies. It breathes like us, it thinks for itself and it has its own personality. It is manipulative, cunning and controlling. This other side of us knows our very thoughts and our feelings. But what makes this addictive side of us so dangerous is that it also knows our past. It knows that we have failed many times in the past, so it just waits inside of us hoping and lurking for the moment of weakness so that it can return to power in our lives. It knows that those moments are coming.

We are addicts for life and our other person knows our emotions and our mental thoughts. My addict was all over me on the 15th when I woke up. It wanted me to use drugs and alcohol. It was trying to take back control over my life. It wanted power back over me. Mentally and physically my very being was being attacked by my addict. However, it was not stronger than my desire not to use. Therefore, I went to so many meetings so that I could remain strong and not use and it worked. I went to about 13 meetings in three and a half days. I called my sponsor and my peers. I talked about what was going on with me in some of those meetings and just listened to other people in other meetings. And after every meeting I felt stronger and stronger. And as I did my addict got weaker and weaker until it decided to let go for now. Please note that my addict is still living inside of me and waiting for another opportunity to attack me. And I had better be ready when it returns or I will loose the battle of sobriety.

For me sobriety is a short term goal and is only being used to get me in position for my ultimate goal. That is to serve my higher power as his servant and slave. This was another reason I was able to defeat my addictive side because I no longer want to do anything to upset my God. I no longer want the Devil laughing in God's face because I did wrong after all that God has done for me. I have received so much of God's undeserved kindness and compassion that it is a shame. My God has always been there for me through both right and wrong. You have read in this book already how much God has done for me and you will read more, because I am not finish telling you about all the interventions in my life.

It is very important to me that I don't hurt God anymore with my wild living and immoral acts. When you are given some many chances over and over even God can loose patience with you. My life has been full of God given opportunities and life saving events again and again.

Life by Suicide teaches us to grow instead of remain. It teaches us to learn from our past and present mistakes and to recognize them as opportunities for growth and change. We learn to feel different about ourselves and to believe that we are willing and able to change our lives for the better. That we no longer have to live in fear as we continue to rid ourselves of all of the vile things that have kept us in our addictions and from the love of God. We learn that God has not left us and that when God is for you, who can be against you. We learn that through honesty there is freedom. We learn in our own hearts and life that old saying! the truth will set you free. It is through the truth that we begin to live our lives as God intended for us. We find that our old secrets have no more power over us when exposed. We come to understand that we too can live happy and joyful lives in according to God's will for us. We are also rewarded by God for our obedience to him.

After my recent attack by my addiction I decided to go to the government center to check on how much money I needed to pay in order to get my driver's license. First of all I have never had a driver's license in my 50 years of living. As a matter of fact I have never even applied for a driver's license in my life. However I decided to change that. So I went to talk with the people at the department of motor vehicles to see what I had to do in order to get my license. After telling the clerk what I needed. She said to me; Mr. Clark my computer shows that you have never had a driver's license before. I told her that was true. She then stated to me how and why did that happen. I, told her about my past life from me going in and out of prison. Also I told her about my long struggle with drugs and alcohol and about me being so unhappy in my life. And, then I told her that I had just recently got out of an impatient treatment program for mental illness and chemical dependency and that I was honestly trying to change my life.

She stated to me that her computer shows that my fines equaled a total of over one thousand eight hundred dollars. She then asked me could I afford to pay that amount, I told her there was no way I would ever be able to pay that amount unless I hit the lottery or was given a payment plan. She then told me that it is within my power to rid you of these fines and I will, so she deleted all of my fines and dues completely out of the system; so that they no longer exist. She then said to me I know it is very hard to change your life after all you have experienced, so this should help make it a little easier. She said now all you have to do is pay for your driver's license. She also gave me a computer prints out, with the states seal on it to show anyone that might question my past records, just in case. I, thanked her and walked out of there thanking and praising God, because I knew without any doubt that his hands were all over this blessing.

Alcohol Anonymous talks about this in it's version of the twelve promises. I was honored to receive such a blessing. My life has been full of pain and suffering and at the same time Jehovah God has always protected me in all of my affairs. I have never been left alone by my God. My love for Jehovah God is strong but my body is weak. My prayers are strong and my spirit is weak.

This is the week of June the 23rd through the 30th and I have had so many problems since I last sat down and wrote on this book. My being is in turmoil because so many people look up to me that I have not been completely honest about my own problems. I have been called the wisest person I have ever met by my counselors, to the greatest friend I have ever had. I have been sought out for my advice and my wisdom so much I have been left alone in my recovery. It feels like that if I share my feelings and thoughts with anybody that I would be letting them down. However, this is nothing new to me it has always been this way for me. People have always looked at me as a leader and have needed me to sustain them.

However this is who I am. All leaders in history had no one to express themselves to but God. And all great leaders fell to the pressure. It is my hopes and prayers that God continue to sustain me. In heaven the arch angel name was Michael, and that is my name. It has been said that Michael's are special. Therefore this will be our next chapter.

CHAPTER FOUR
Michael's are Special

Earlier this week a music icon died from what is believed to have been a heart attack. This young man has always been in my mind and in my heart. Not because I loved his music even though I did, but because what he represented to me. It was because of our parallel lives that we lived. I was born in Gary, Indiana just as he was. I was born in the year of 1958 just as he was. My name is Michael, just as his name was Michael. My mother is a Jehovah Witness just as his mother is. We are both fifty years old and yet we lived two different lives. I've always wondered all of my life how he turned out to be this great music icon full of fame and fortune and I turned out to be this alcoholic dope-fin. I've always wondered how this was possible. I have said to myself did God love him more than he loved me. Therefore raising him to fame and fortune and leaving me to the dumps of Gary, Ind. I've said to myself so many times how could he have turned out to be the person that he is and me the person that I am.

I have admired this young man all of my childhood life and all of my adulthood life. I always knew that his parents could have not loved him any more that my parents loved me. There had to be some higher source that allowed him to excel and caused me to fail. What was it that God loved about him that God didn't love about me? How was this possible I have always loved God and talked about him to other people? I have always prayed and asked God to forgive me of my sins. I have always said my prayers to him and glorified his name. My love for God has always been strong regardless of the many crimes I have committed. Could this be the reason that God excelled him and left me to ruins? No, this could not be the reason because God judges a man's heart and my heart has always been pure. I've always wondered if this other Michael even had the time to pray to God with all of his fame and fortune. Traveling all over the world and being able to do and buy whatever he wanted too. I wondered if he even recognized God any longer.

However, that could not be it either because from what the media has said about this man he was very close to his mother. And, his mother is a Jehovah Witness, so I assume he loved Jehovah too. What had him living so well and me living in my pain and suffering all of these years?

I have used so much crack cocaine that I have been rushed to the hospital for chest pains and have had two heart attacks. And yet God has sustained me but allowed him to past from just one heart attack. Let me say right now that I loved this man and he didn't even know I was alive and had these feelings and thoughts. He has always been an inspiration to me and I have always thought of him as my role model to better myself. So, please show some honor and respect for this man and not misunderstand what I am saying. I, have nothing but the utmost respect for him and all of his accomplishments. This is not a statement of jealousy or resentment but one of admiration. It is only to express and outline my feelings and thoughts about how my live turned out compared to his. This comparison is only being used to complete Live by Suicide and because it has been my truth all of my life. My point is where do I go from here? I will tell you this that even in his death he has inspired me to continue in my work by finish writing this book. The thing that came to me yesterday while speaking of this gentleman was that he used the gift that God gave him all the days of his life and I did not use the gifts that God gave me.

My gift was given to me at the very same age his was. My gift was to spread the good news of God. Even as a paperboy I did this but didn't follow through like he did. I guess I needed to come full circle. I guess I had more lessons to learn and more experiences to live. But as I said earlier in this book that God's plan and purpose can not go uncompleted, so therefore I live.

Life By Suicide

At this point I would like to extend my sorrow and heart felt love to his family during this time of hardship. And say may Almighty God continue to bless your family. In hopes that I did not say anything in this book about your beloved son and brother that caused you any discomfort.

My struggle to live a life of comfort according to God's will is still in the makings. But as I told you earlier you would be watching a man commit suicide while reading this book. And I assure you that by the time this book is completed, I Michael Clark will be dead to my old self and I will live a life through Life by Suicide. This was the sole purpose of this book to kill the old Michael through truth and to rid myself of all the things that have caused me to struggle. I am so tired of being unhappy and not feeling good about myself that my only way out is to kill myself. Drugs and alcohol does not make me happy, nor does over-eating. These things are no more than substitutes for the real problems in my life.

We have mental, emotional and physical disorders and problems. Medications can help us to stabilize ourselves; but the real solution is with our relationship with God. We are not living the way God intended for us and we are out of sink with God. Our only opportunity to find happiness is through God, for us there is no other way. Therefore, we must rid ourselves of all that is evil and vile in us. We must face ourselves with the truth and then arm ourselves with God's purpose for us. None of our electrical devices will work for us until we plug them into an electrical outlet or socket. They were created too only work through the use of electricity. We are no different when it comes to our lives. We can no more function in a happy state without our creator.

That is why I seat alone over and over wishing that I was not the person that I am. And yet I find that the happiest time in my life is when I'm thinking about all the things I can do to change my life. And, yet I do nothing about it. But while in that state of mind I feel hopeful and grateful about all the things that I could do only if I was happy. Knowing that I could be happy and live in happiness is and so far only been a dream to me. And yet I desire it so much. My very soul wishes for happiness and my very spirit grieves for it with everything within my being. I long so much for the love and grace of happiness. I dream of the day that I will die if that what it takes to be happy. I pray that God gives me some days of happiness before I do die. That is the whole purpose of this book to kill myself so that I can finally live in that state of joy. That very state of happiness that our forefather's gave to the power of Satan and that God gave back to us through the giving of his son Jesus Christ.

I'm talking about that happiness that we didn't even know that we were naked, and we felt no shame in it. Our forefather's then disobeyed God and we are paying the price for it right now in our unhappiness. It is like leaving a will for your children when you die. Unfortunately our forefather's left us a death sentence. That is the state of separation from our creator and the state of looking for love in all the wrong places. That is the state of mind and spirit that we have as creatures that are separated from the one who designed them in the very first place. We are stuck in that very state of looking for the other part of ourselves that we can't find.

I watched the memorial services for this music icon on my television all day yesterday and was amazed. First of all I truly had no idea how large this man was to the world. I knew that he was famous but what I didn't know was how huge he was in life. I have never seen anything like that in my entire life. This man was loved throughout the entire world. Michael's memorial services was reportedly watched by close to a billion people all over the world and the Staple Center was full to capacity over seventeen thousand people. It seemed if though the world stopped completely during his funeral.

I watched wondering if ten people outside my family would show for my memorial service. This thought brought tears to my heart. I have been living in Minneapolis for sixteen years and yet when I pretended to be dead no one came to even comfort my daughter. The only concern I received was, where is my seventeen dollars worth of food stamps? This man was loved for more than just his music he was loved for what inspiration he gave to people all over the world. You can not ever be that large of a person without having Almighty God's intervention.

The amount of superstars within their own rights paid tribute to this man. I was so inspired that I watched every show and channel that I could. You have to understand something here, for me to show that much love and concern about anything is amazing. I have been so unhappy and depressed with my own life and problems that I don't give a dam about anything else. However this year alone I have been inspired by two Black men, first the first Black President of the United States and now by Michael. These two men by the grace of God, has taught me that to show your face is the essence of love. And that is what I am doing in this book, showing my face. For that lesson alone I am grateful.

When I look at Michael I see the use of the full potential that God gave to him and he used every bit of it. When I look at myself I see the failure to completely use all that God gave to me. My gift from God was the gift to teach the word of God and I failed to do that on a world wide scale. I've always talked to people about God that I ran into on a one on one basis.

Sometimes I look at these so called television evangelist and just shake my head because of all the false things they teach about God and his son Jesus Christ. I know that these things are not true because the Bible does not teach these things and yet people believe them. The amount of money these people make in the name of God is ridiculous. However, they will pay for that when judgment day arrives. My point is that I have not filled my obligation to God for the gift that he gave to me. And that is the main reason I've been so unhappy. I vividly remember wanting to be a civil rights leader or a preacher and my fears and failures caused me to give up on my dreams. Hopefully this book is the beginning of that dream.

One of those fears is what people would say about me and my past. Also the fear of being murdered by white society, and the government, as we all know that every time a Black man exceeds slavery they have been know to kill us. It is their history. However, I am about to show my face; so if that is what they are going to do, so be it. My time has come and that is all it is to it.

Michael was a gift to this world from God rather you believe it or not. However what is between Michael and God is between Michael and God.

There are people in this world that work for Satan the Devil. People whose main purpose in life is to destroy everything good that God brings to earth .They are put here only to hurt and cause confusion to those that love God. These people spread their vicious stories and opinions based on what they believe and could care less who they hurt and why. Their only purpose is to gather ratings and popularity. They hide their true purpose behind the freedom of the press. You have these people running around with their cameras in front of your home immediately after it has burned to the ground asking people who have lost everything, how do you feel? They come to you after your child has been kidnapped and raped wanting to know how it feels. They come to your home and want to know what does it feel like having both of your parents murdered by a robber? They have no honor and respect in what they do. They could care less about your time to grieve. Their only purpose is to seek out pain and suffering and report the out come. They pretend to be doing their job and to that there is nothing wrong with that type of work.

However where is the compassion and understanding? Where is the concern for those who are living? Where is the spirit in which they come? They come with hateful questions and hateful answers. They come to us as drug dealers with no regards for anybody except for themselves. They sell the same hate and chemical as drug dealers. They are no different in any way. They might not cause people to commit crimes and do other things that drugs do to people, but the same amount of damage is done on an emotional and physical level. As an addict and alcoholic I know from experience what damage is done on an emotional and spiritual level by the use of chemicals. The media's chemical or substance is more dangerous than that of alcohol or drugs. The Bible even talks about how evil and injurious the tongue is to mankind, (a unruly injurious thing it is full of death dealing poison) James 3; 8. And if you continue to read chapter 9 and 10 you will see out of the same mouth comes blessings and curses. The Bible further says that it is not proper for these things to go on occurring this way. This is the same wickedness and evilness that occurs with the media. They sell death dealing poison, drug dealers; as I said.

And just like drug dealers it is all for money. What good hearted God fearing person would come to you after you have been through a major ordeal or death of a loved one. With all kinds of off the wall questions while you are grieving, with cameras and crews to show the pain and suffering of another human being. I, tell you let one of their family members get killed and you will not see media trucks and cameras in front of their homes. At that point they will show each other professional courtesy. That proves that it is not just doing their job, but rather following instructions from their earthly father, Satan the devil.

I have seen the love that was given by this icon to this world and I say may God bless him and his family. And just to answer some of your evil questions like, who's going to get the children and where is the body? The answer is none of your damn business. The question is where are you going to bury your child when the time comes? And believe me it's coming for all of us. What we all should have learned from Michael is this; "courage is the bypass cowards need to know." Last but certainly not least rest in peace Michael and know that Almighty God has arrived.

My hope is that I can find some happiness through Life by Suicide. It is my only chance that I rid my life of all the evil and veil things in my life and in my heart and past. My goal is to find God through the Bible and through prayer while being honest about the sins I have committed. To show my face in order to find the love I need to be happy. The Bible says to humble yourselves therefore, under the mighty hand of God, that he may exalt you in due time. Therefore I am throwing all of my burdens and cares into the hands of the lord. And could care less how man attacks me from this day forward.

My secrets will be revealed in this book and it does not matter to me who knows them or use them. I would only suggest that a person use them to better their own life or as a guide to follow. And not use them to seek hateful propaganda, but if you choose too be my guest. Just know that my secrets are toxic and can be very deadly for they have kept me so unhappy for fifty years. So be very careful carrying my secrets from one place to another or even from one person to another, if used for the wrong purpose. You might find yourself on drugs wondering what the hell happened.

This book is my blessing from God and can be used to help those who suffer as I do. But for those using it to hurt others it can be their curse. The reason that I stated being careful is because sometimes people take other people experiences and make fun or jokes out of them. I've learned in the past that the same thing that will make you laugh will also make you cry.

This morning my daughter had to be at work at 5; 00 am and I decided to get up and walk her to work. She is only 16 yrs. old and although we live four blocks from her job it is still not safe for a child that age to be out that early in the morning. I saw the joy in her face that I was thinking about her enough to get up and walk her to work without her asking me. In the past either because of my selfishness or my depression this would more than likely not have happened. As we walked to her job the first person we saw was an older man that just appeared out of the bushes from nowhere as through he was looking to stalk somebody. My daughter even commented, what is he doing and where did he come from? I told her there is no telling what he is doing and for her to just keep walking. Then within the same block I saw a person that I used to get high off of drugs with, she was so high that she didn't even know who I was. She more than likely was out all night prostituting and wanted to know if I wanted to buy a silver necklace. Keep in mind that it is about 4:45 am. My daughter once again asked me what is she doing out here this early in the morning. Therefore I told her that she probably was out here selling her body for drugs. I believe for the first time my daughter realized what I had been telling her about the dangers of the streets. I tell her all the time that the freaks come out at night.

This lady that was prostituting herself was seeking shelter from a long night of drug use. And even through she didn't recognize me I still could have helped her. However she had stolen from me the last time I saw her and therefore I looked the other way. What goes around comes around, the same thing that will make you laugh will also make you cry.

I remember robbing this place for drug money and while using drugs I thought that it was so funning how the people acted when I had my gun in their faces. The amount of fear and the lack of control they had knowing that their lives were in my hands. However it was

Life By Suicide

not so funning when two months later someone robbed me at gun point. I had the very same fear and lack of control knowing that my life was in the hands of this person. Once again the same things that will make you laugh will also make you cry. Keep that in mind when using the information in this book to try and hurt some one. I have been through a lot of pain and suffering to get to this point in my life. There is nothing funning about the physical and mental abuse I've taken myself through. Not to even mention the emotional suffering and social problems that I have suffered through. My relationship with God has suffered along with that of my family including my child.

Therefore my need to be honest about my past is the only way for me to commit suicide. It is my time to shine and follow the path written for me by God. He has sustained me through all of these trails and errors. I can no longer live without being who I truly am. It is time to show my face. As I said earlier courage is the by pass cowards need to know.

I will no longer be a coward to my past. I will no longer hide my face in fear that you might not like me. I will no longer be the face of some one who is not living in my skin. I will no longer pretend to be someone whom my spirit disagrees with. But what I am willing to do is live my life standing on holy ground. You see that our bodies are the temples of God. And those temples are holy, we become unholy because we do not live in harmony with that temple. Therefore creating new faces that the world sees but not as who we truly are. We change our holy temple to create what we think and feel is best for us to live in our own environment.

Therefore changing the course of our lives and the plan God had made out for us. This should come to you as no surprise when you look at the course Adam and Eve took. They changed the natural course of their holy temples to create what they thought would better fit their environment. Which was to know what is good and what is not. They were told that they would become like God's themselves, therefore they disobeyed their original God given holy temple. They ended up creating new faces for themselves totally against the essences of God's love. So you see that when we disobey our creator we actually change who we are. Our temples are no longer holy. I don't know how old Adam and Eve was at the time they disobeyed God. But if we consider our own life time experiences it would be safe to say that they were teenagers.

Also considering how long mankind lived in those days the age of fifty to even one hundred could be consider as teenagers. In our own life time this is the age in which our children decide that they no longer need our guidance and that they are old enough to make their own decisions. At this point we begin to change the course of our parents will for us. This is no different than what our fore father and fore mother did when they disobeyed God. They changed the course of our existence. Therefore we became imperfect human beings. And the very first thing that we did was to try and create a new face to fit into our new environment.

How did they do that? Well they tried to cover up their nakedness. The environment in general had not changed even through they were put out the Garden of Eden. Their temple was no longer holy and therefore they had to create a new face to feel comfortable in the very same environment.

Let me see if I can give you another example of what I truly mean. Take a child that was born in the suburbs and move that child into a low income housing project. Where there are gangs and drugs and all sorts of violence and viciousness. In order for that child to survive that child would need to become some thing that they are not in order to just live a daily life. Otherwise they would end up being prey to everyone in the community. Walking down the street everyday would become a nightmare for that child. That child would have to change his face in order to live comfortable, becoming just as violent as the environment. Adam's change was to find and make clothing. He realized that he was naked. Just think it never bothered him before he disobeyed God. At the time of his living accordingly to God's will he never thought of his nakedness being a problem. He changed his face to fit his new environment.

It was my purpose to make this book as short as possible and at the same time give as much information as possible for you to commit suicide. I believe that that has been accomplished for this chapter. Therefore let's move to the next chapter.

However before we do let me tell you another intervention from Almighty God that saved my life. Using this as an example will help you understand the term undeserved kindness. Undeserved means that you have not earned anything. It means that you did not work for what you received. It means that it was given to you freely without any effort from you. It means that somebody cared for you without your asking they fulfilled a need of yours. The word kindness we all know the meaning. But for those that don't the dictionary, says "wanting and liking to do good to bring happiness to others'. So, undeserved kindness would mean that someone wanted to do something for you without you having to work for it.

I was living in Portland, Oregon at the time and had been using drugs. My money had run out but my addiction to crack cocaine was still alive and well. Therefore in order to feed my drug habit I had to commit a crime in order to get more money. Therefore I robbed a place for the cash that I needed. Before I was able to completely get out of the neighborhood in which I committed the crime police were everywhere. Therefore I began running as fast as I possibly could to escape the crime scene. However I was spotted by a police officer and the chase began. This officer must have chased me for at least a block and a half before I lost him. However I still needed to get out of the niegborhood. The thing that allowed me to loose the police officer was that there was some construction work being done at the time and there were signs everywhere stating do not enter. I believe that the police officer obeyed the construction signs and I didn't. And that is what allowed me to loose him.

However, I was still running as hard as I could. Once again for the second time in my life I heard that same familiar voice. The voice I spoke about earlier in another intervention. The voice that was so powerful and demanding that it allowed no room for thinking. It was that same voice that controlled my actions from its intense power. The voice from before that put fear in my very being. As I was told by this voice in these exact words, Michael Stop Now! The very moment I stopped running and began walking. I realized that I was on an unfinished bridge about four hundred feet in the air. I had run through the construction signs that warned the public about this bridge. I assume the police officer knew that and that is why he never came that way looking for me. Had I not paid attention to that voice I would have run straight to my death. I was so over whelmed that, that is where I spend the night on that bridge. I sat there until daylight thanking God because I knew without any reasonable doubt that he had intervened in my life and saved me one more time. I was so grateful that I left the money that I had stolen on that bridge and walked away. This is the ultimate example of undeserved kindness. By no means did I deserve the kindness that I received that night. First of all I had been using drugs and second I had just committed a crime.

The Bible says to treat your body with the utmost care for it is the temple of the Holy Spirit. Also the Bible says that thou shall not steal. Clearly I had broken both of these laws. I can only say that God loved me even when I was doing wrong. He knew that he had a purpose for my life and that his word and plans cannot fall short of coming true.

It is through this undeserved kindness that I am here today. May all glory and praises go directly to Jehovah God. Praise his holy name.

CHAPTER FIVE
Working and Fighting For Salvation

Let me start off by stating to you that salvation is our ultimate goal. Salvation comes through one source and one source only. There is no other name under heaven or earth that we can receive salvation through. That name is Jesus Christ our Lord and savior. All power and glory was given unto him by Almighty God who has all power. You can not receive salvation through any other name, period, with no exceptions. Listen, here is a Bible verse that explains it pure and simple, (Colossians 1; 13-20) it reads as followed "he delivered us from the authority of the darkness and transferred us into the kingdom of the son of his love, 14; by means of whom we have our release by ransom the forgiveness of our sins. 15; he is the image of the invisible god, the firstborn of all creation; 16; because by means of him all (others) things were created in the heavens and upon the earth, the things visible and the things invisible, no matter whether they are thrones or lordships or governments or authorities. All (other) things have been created through him and for him. 17; also he is before all other things and by means of him all other things were made to exist. 18; and he is the head of the body, the congregation. He is the beginning, the first born from the dead. That he might become the one who is first in all things; 19; because (god) saw good for all fullness to dwell in him. 20; and through him to reconcile again to himself all other things by making peace through the blood he shed on the torture stake, no matter whether they are the things upon the earth or the things in heavens".

It is through Jesus Christ that we have our only opportunity through the undeserved kindness to receive salvation. Now this salvation was not given to us because we deserved it. No, it was given to us through the grace of God; because he loved us so much. Not because we loved him but because he loved us. There is nothing that we could have done and there is nothing that we can do to ever deserve this salvation. However, through this undeserved kindness in which we have received salvation we now have the right to gain this salvation through our faith in our lord and savior Jesus Christ.

Webster's dictionary describes salvation as the saving of a person from sin, then it goes on to say, something that saves as well as, the saving from danger and evil. Last night while dozing off to sleep I wondered to myself about the ultimate sacrifice a person would have to make to save some one from sin. Well that sacrifice for us was the torture stake that Jesus endured. Understand this that to boldly and meekly lay your life down for the saving of another human being is the greatest thing that a person can ever do. And very few of us are willing to lay our lives down to save the life of someone we don't even know. However, many of us would be willing to die for our children's sake but for a total stranger it would be difficult.

If I had to choose between my child and some one else's child there would be nothing to think about. I would save my child without any doubt. But God having created us chose to give us salvation through his son's death. Do you not realize that God could have just created something else to serve his purpose? He is the creator of all things yet he gave his son. Do you know of anyone that would do that? That kind of love is unimaginable. Therefore we are obligated to receive salvation on God's love for us alone. We have done nothing to deserve it for it was given to us freely. Although we received this gift freely we can only truly have it by our faith in Jesus Christ. Because it is through our faith that this undeserved kindness is available to us.

Faith is the things hoped for but yet not seen. Faith also is of no use without works. In order to receive or hope for something you haven't yet seen. You would have to first believe that it is real. Therefore through this belief your hope lives but if you do not believe there can be no faith in which that you hope for. Once again proving that faith without works is dead. Through our faith we work for our hope. And it is through this work we receive that in which

Life By Suicide

we believe. Now that our faith has worked our hope and belief we then receive what is unseen. What is unseen in our case would be the salvation that Jesus Christ offers us. Our work to this faith would be to live as Christ did when he took on human form. And that would be to rid ourselves of all the corrupt and vile things in our lives. That means striving for being Christ like. What are some of those vile things? Well God's word the Bible says that the work of the flesh is manifest, and they are fornication, uncleanness, loose conduct. Idolatry, practice of spiritism , enmities, strife, jealousy, fits of anger, contentions, division sects, envies, drunken bouts, revelries, and things like these. And for some of us if not all of us there are other things that are holding us back from receiving our salvation. Things like gambling, overeating, drugs and alcohol, being disobedience to our parents, the lack of respect for others. It is all of those shameful things that we talked about earlier in this book.

We as addicts of all these things above, already look forward to the day that we will be saved from our pain because of these things. Therefore we need to work to receive our salvation given to us freely. We need to get rid of everything that is killing us. For me there goes the drugs and alcohol. For you, you already know for yourself exactly what these things are. You might say if salvation was given to us freely then why is it a need to work for it. You first must believe that your salvation is possible and it is through belief that we work. We will only work for it only if we believe. The Bible says that "the father loves the son and has given all things into his hands, he that exercises faith in the son has everlasting life. He that disobeys the son will not see life, but the wrath of God remains upon him".

To exercise faith in Jesus is to do the will of his father who sent him. We can not exercise faith in Jesus through murder, theft, drunkenness, overeating, fornication, lying stealing and all of the other things that the father says we shall not do. Therefore we must work on ridding ourselves of such things.

If you are a thief that means stop stealing. If you commit fornication, that means stop committing fornication. If you are a murderer that means don't kill. For me that means stop using drugs. Alcohol and drugs have stopped me from reaching my salvation. Therefore I went to treatment in order to exercise faith that in the hope that I could stay clean and sober from the use of drugs that I might receive my salvation. The treatment center was both the work and the faith. The hope was through the treatment center because I believed that it would help me to rid myself of these vile things. I never would have gone to treatment if I did not believe that it would help me. That belief exercised my faith and that faith brought upon my hope. So that if I believed that treatment would help me to rid myself of drugs and alcohol then I would go. By going my work and faith brought about the hope that I would receive salvation from my alcohol and drug addiction. Remember that the dictionary says also that salvation is the saving of something from danger or evil. I hoped by going to treatment it would save me from the dangers and evil of using drugs and alcohol.

From this point on you will have to figure out how to work your faith so that you will receive your hope. Faith without work is dead. Sometimes salvation can be given to us by our lord Christ Jesus through another human being. Simply because all things has been given unto him. We will call this type of salvation earthly salvation.

I remember when I was about 16 years old. Two friends and I committed several different kinds of crime all through the night. All night we drank alcohol and took whatever we wanted from people we didn't know. As we were leaving one crime scene to go to the next crime scene. The police picked up our trail. However by now we were in two different stolen cars. The police was now in hot pursuit of us. As they chased the car we had just stolen, the other stolen car they knew nothing about. We had stolen that car from a different county. As the police chased the car just stolen they drove right pass the older stolen car. To make a long story short one of us was caught and two of us got away. The one person that was caught received ten years of prison time. And although the one person caught was given the opportunity to have his prison sentence cut in half if he was willing to tell on the other people with him. He never told on me or the other person and served those ten years in my behalf.

Salvation was given to me through this one friend by keeping me away from the dangers of prison life. Not to many years later I

Life By Suicide

would serve time in prison for a friend of mine. So you see that we can receive salvation from an earthly source and even that was God's purpose. Salvation on this scale is in no way a comparison to the type of salvation on a heavenly scale that Jesus Christ did. This earthly salvation is only to save us from something that we could not handle or deal with at the time. Neither myself or my other friend could have dealt with prison at that time, the person who served time was the only one of us that could have handled prison and came out a man. So my salvation was through the giving of someone's life in order for me to not be in danger. God does not go back on his plans at anytime for any reason. And all my life since then I have thanked this guy in my heart, thoughts and mind. I always knew that God had intervened in my life once again.

Now back to working for our salvation. The amount of work we put into ridding ourselves of the dangers of sin in our lives. Is according to the amount of faith that we have in our hopes! You see I hope not to use drugs and alcohol for the rest of my life. That is why I went to treatment. I also hope not to die from drugs and alcohol, that's another reason I put my works into action so that my faith would led to the activation of my hopes. I hope to be saved by Jesus Christ since all things are in his hand. My faith in his salvation for me forced a reaction in my hopes. That is through my works I might be saved. This concept may seem difficult but believe me it is very simple. If you hope for something but you do not believe in your hopes, then your works will not manifest. It is because you do not believe therefore you do not work towards your hope. There is nothing on this earth that we don't have to work for. Rather that is food, clothing or shelter. We also have to work on our relationships with others and on our marriages. The amount of work we put in determines the quality of our hopes. Let's just say that you hope to buy yourself a new car. You first have to believe that you can save enough money to buy that car. And if you don't start saving for your (hope) the new car. Then having that new car will not happen. Because the work you put into the car was not enough to salvage your hopes. But if we believe in our hopes we will activate our faith through our works, so that our hopes will become a reality.

Our pain is why we need to work on our salvation. It is very painful living under the gasp of alcohol and drugs. It has to be painful to be over weight and not feel good about how you look and not being able to participate in certain things. It must be painful to work forty hours a week and loose all of your money at the casino in three hours because of your gambling addiction. It must be painful to live in the state of depression in your own little dark world. It must be painful not be happy in any endeavor. You alone have to decide to work on your salvation.

For many years I refused to believe that I was a person who suffered from chronic depression. Therefore I stayed in the constant world of my own darkness. Having no hopes of ever relieving myself from it. Because I didn't want to believe that I was depressed I put forth no works to rid myself of my depression, so I lived in it. Then after going to treatment and being told that in order for me to remain clean from drugs and alcohol. I would also have to treat my depression.

At this point I became willing to believe that I was depressed and began to work on it. I worked on it by going to see a psychiatrist, then I furthered my works by taking the medications he prescribed. As well as keeping my future appointments. And it was through my belief that in order for me to rid myself of drugs and alcohol I would have to deal with my depression. This work brought forth my hopes which became a reality. I am no longer depressed because of my faith. The hope of being clean from drugs and alcohol has become a reality. Now my salvation is reachable through my belief. Faith is the things hoped for but yet not seen.

If we can work for our addictions then we can also work to rid ourselves from these addictions. That's right we have worked hard to stay in our addictions. Being depressed and not getting out of bed because you have no energy is working for your addiction. Stealing to acquire drugs is also working for our addiction. Low self esteem is working for our addiction. Eating while unhappy is working for our addiction. All of the things that we do or don't do, we work for our addictions. When we do nothing to get us out of our unhappiness we are working for our addictions. I know that I have worked over time for my addictions. And I am not just talking about illegal crimes.

I'm also talking about all the days in bed because I was so depressed. I'm talking about all the negative thoughts that have kept me from believing in myself. I'm talking about all the suicidal thoughts and the many gallons of tears. I'm talking about all of the self defeating behaviors. I'm also talking about all the lies and deceit. I'm talking about being irresponsible. The list goes on and on. So know that if we can work that hard to stay unhappy surely we can work just as hard to be happy.

Life by Suicide teaches us that we need to kill off all of these negative behaviors so that we can live. Life by Suicide teaches us to believe that our salvation is real through our work of ridding ourselves of all the vile things in our lives. Life by Suicide teaches us to work for our salvation. Life by Suicide teaches us how to work for the brutal truth so that we can rid ourselves of all wickedness. It is through these teaching that we can look forward to happiness.

Unhappiness is the state of mind from the devil. Happiness is the state of mind from God and our salvation through his son Jesus Christ. You can not serve God in an unhappy state of mind, body and soul. However by the undeserved kindness, indeed, you have been saved through faith. And this is not of owning to you, it is God's gift to us. For the Bible says in the book of Ephesians chapter two verses 3 through 5 that" yes, among them we all at one time conducted ourselves and in harmony with the desires of our flesh, doing the things willed by the flesh and the thoughts and we were naturally children of wrath even as the rest. But god, who is rich in mercy, for his great love with which he loved us. Made us alive together with the Christ, even when we were dead in trespasses by undeserved kindness you have been saved". So we have the grand opportunity to change our lives and receive that salvation. As I told you earlier in this book that nothing can keep us from the love of God. So don't let these little bitty things of the flesh continue to control your life.

At the very beginning of this book I spoke about how much I hated myself and how much pain that I was in, because of that hate. But through my faith in Jehovah God and his son Jesus Christ I kept on trying regardless of all my mistakes and failures. I refused to give up on my hope of salvation from drugs and alcohol. After thirty six years of alcohol abuse and through eight treatment centers my work has relieved me of my hopelessness. My work was going to treatment because I hoped that they would help me. After eighteen years of drug abuse my faith has given me hope that I might remain clean from drugs. And as long as I continue to work I will continue to stay sober.

Our work will determine the outcome of our salvation. After thirty five years of depression my work because of my hope has set me free because of my faith. About ten years ago I was diagnosed with chronic depression. At that time in my life I believed that depression was the state of mind by weak people, and I certainly didn't believe that Black people got depressed. I don't even think the word depression was ever used in my household as a child. Depression to me was just having a bad day. And if it lasted to long it was just a part of life considering the situation I was in.

Therefore I had no belief in what this doctor told me ten years ago. Depression was not even a consideration. Therefore I didn't work for it because I had no belief in it. Therefore I stayed depressed for another ten years. I however did believe that Black people did not get depressed and that depression was a White man's sickness. But when you think about it and the medical term of situational depression Black people are actually at the top of the list. Situational depression is caused by the situation that you are in. And once your situation goes away so does your depression. Well Black people's situation has lasted for over four hundred years, considering the pain and suffering that we have been through in this country. And that situation for the masses of us has not changed. Our depression has been from one generation to the next generation.

However, today I do know that I am depressed. Therefore I did something about it through my belief my faith allowed my work to exist and my hopes became my reality. Let's keep moving on.

Now we need to talk about fighting for your salvation. Our fighting for salvation is different from working for salvation. Now that we have worked for our salvation our lives have changed. We are no longer depressed. We are no longer gamblers. We are no longer over eaters. We no longer fornicate. We no longer killers. We no longer get drunk or use drugs. We are no longer the person that we used to be regardless of what that was. You now know by now the things that you yourselves need to get rid of. I have explained them to you throughout this book. And since we are no longer our old self we have to fight to keep it that way.

Every time that I went to treatment I stayed away from drugs and alcohol for some period of time. But I always ended up using again. Because the work I did in treatment was not the work I did once I got out of treatment. I stopped doing what I was suppose to. The very things that got me sober. Once sober and feeling good about myself I stopped working on myself. Because I believed that I was already saved from my addictions through the work I had put in while in treatment. Shortly after I stopped working for my sobriety I began using again.

Therefore all of the things that I went to treatment for became my reality once again. I believed that drugs and alcohol was the reason for me not liking myself. I believed that it was the reason I was so unhappy. I believed that alcohol and drugs would control my destiny. I believed that my life was not worth living and began to have suicidal thoughts once again. My self esteem dropped to its lowest point ever. And once again my life was back in the dark world of loneliness and unhappiness. My world was once again in the very hands of nothingness. And my motivation to do anything about it was gone. The only hope that I had was my mental abilities to believe that God would save me again once I went to him. My childhood faith that God loves me kept me believing that I could rise out of the dark world I was now living in.

It was that belief that slowly got me to my feet and out of bed. That same faith allowed me to believe that I could once again get clean through work. My work said treatment. Treatment was the help I needed. My hope became my reality. Alcohol and drugs are just symptoms of a deeper problem. That problem is unhappiness. Unhappiness comes from the separation from God. So my going back to treatment again and again was my fighting for my salvation.

I don't know if you have ever heard this story before but it is the perfect example of fighting for your salvation. Two mice got themselves got in a bucket of sour cream. Realizing that they were about to drown and die they began to paddle their way out. After a while one of the mice decided that there was no way they would ever be able to get out of the sour cream, because it was to soft. Therefore the mice gave up because it said to it's self, I would rather just die than continue to suffer. So it quit paddling his feet and died. The other mice refused to die and it paddled so hard and for so long that the sour cream turned into butter and the mice just walked out the bucket and lived.

So you decide which mice you want to be. Do you want to give up on your salvation and die or do you want to fight for your salvation and live. I would like to work and fight for my salvation and live.

Fighting for salvation is nothing more than working hard through the struggles you will go through even though you are saved. Fighting for your salvation means keep getting up every time that you fall. Fighting for your salvation means that you are willing to do what it takes to continue to be saved. The only way to loose is by quitting. Because you have to remember that this salvation was given to us freely. We inherited it through the undeserved kindness from a loving God. So all we have to do is to have faith that our salvation exist.

Moses the biblical man, fought for his salvation by taken on the appointed job of delivering the children of Israel out of Egypt. These people were hard headed and full of complaints. But Moses believed that God would do as he said and Moses kept on fighting. The Bible called the children of Israel a stiffed neck people and God wanted to wipe them off the face of the earth. However Moses kept praying for them and praying. Moses, of course through God lead these people through the dessert for forty years because they would not obey God.

Abraham fought for his salvation by going to a place he had no idea where he was going. But his faith that God would do what he said he would do lead him to work for his salvation. Imagine the pain knowing that you have to sacrifice your only child. Can you realize the emotional turmoil he felt. Can you even imagine the thought process of walking your child into the mountains knowing that you are about to sacrifice him? And your child asking you father where are we going. Abraham had already been saved because God had already told him that his off springs would be like the sands on the sea and no man would be able to count them in numbers. Because of the faith that Abraham had in God's word he fought through all of his pains and feelings for his salvation.

Job fought hard and long for his salvation and suffered without end. I could go on and on about the people in the Bible that fought for their salvation because they believed God would do what he said he would.

Saul, who persecuted the followers of Jesus, once he was saved fought hard and long for his salvation. His named was changed to Paul and he suffered and fought harder for his salvation from Saul to Paul.

Jesus Christ also worked for his salvation being the son of God. It was through his work that God exalted him to a higher position. The Bible says in the book of Hebrews chapter one verse nine "you loved righteousness and you hated lawlessness. That is why God, your God, anointed you with the oil of exultation more than your partner. More than that, when he found himself in fashion as a man. He humbled himself and became obedient as far as death, yes death on a torture stake. For this very reason also God exalted him to a superior position and kindly gave him the name that is above every other name, so that in the name of Jesus every knee should bend of those in heaven and those on earth and those under the ground. And every tongue should openly acknowledge that Jesus Christ is Lord to the glory of God the father".

The great thing about having Jesus as our only road to salvation is that he has lived what we are going through. He has put his faith to work that his hopes became his reality. He knows what we are feeling. Imagine being a superior being and then come among the very thing that you created. To have the things that you created talk about you and try to kill you and ultimately murder you. Speaking of putting in work for your salvation no one has put more work in than this man, Jesus. If you were to look in the book of Hebrews 4; 15 and 16 you would read "for we have as high priest, not one who cannot sympathize with our weaknesses, but one who has been tested in all respects like ourselves, but without sin".

Therefore we need to put the work and fight into the safety of our salvation. We cannot be excused from our lack of faith. And through this faith let our works introduce us to the reality of our hope. In the days of his flesh Jesus offered up supplications and also petitions to the one who was able to save him out of death, with strong outcries and tears, and he was favorably heard for his godly fear, Hebrews 5;7. So let us not fear the hard things that we need to change in our lives because the one person that offers salvation has gone through our pain too. Let us continue to fight for our right to receive salvation.

Life by Suicide is my way of continuing to fight for my salvation. After trying so many other things and falling short over and over again. I decided that I wanted to kill myself. However, my love for my daughter stopped those thoughts because I knew that I could not leave her in this world by herself. This is how I actually came up with the concept of Life by Suicide. All of my life experiences and my love for God gave me this new idea. I could kill myself and yet live. My fight for happiness through salvation has been a long drawn out process. Besides the drugs and alcohol there also was the depression. There have been weight problems and health problems. My fight has been full of pain and suffering. And the most pain is the one of loneliness. I tell people all the time that there are worst things on this earth than death. And I can promise you that loneliness is one of them.

I spoke earlier about alcohol being the main reason that I was separated from my family. Therefore I have lived on this earth for fifty years and for thirty five of those years I have been alone. Well I did live in Seattle where my oldest sister lives for about eight years. But I can truly tell you that to be alone is devastating. To have no body to love leaves you without anybody loving you. To walk through life by yourself is one of the worst things that I have ever felt. You can't trust anyone because they are not family. Because when it is all said and done family is all that you have.

When I think about grown men that do not take care of their own children, my heart aches! I knew that if for any reason the mother of my child and I were to break up my child was going to be with me. And if not I definitely was going to be a part of her life. The lack of love leads to one thing, loneliness.

Imagine what Jesus went through trying to give us salvation. This man had disciples and great crowds of people around him while he performed all sorts of miracles. People knew that this man was of God. The disciples for sure knew that he was the son of the living God. And at the time of his death one disciple betrayed him. The rest of them ran off and left him. And the only one that followed him to see what was going to happen, denied three times that he even knew Jesus. Out of all the people that he healed from their sicknesses and all of the miracles alone, you would think that somebody would have shown up to support him. And if for no other reason just to see if there would be another miracle.

However, the only ones there were his accusers and his family. Could you imagine the hurt that he must have felt? And yet he said forgive them father for they know not what they do. The work and the fighting that Jesus put in for salvation is the reason there is no other name on this earth or in heaven that can give us salvation. And on top of that he still did not charge us for our salvation. It was through undeserved kindness that we are saved. For the undeserved kindness of God which brings salvation to all sorts of men was manifested. It must have been very lonely for Jesus. Listen, I know that we have all had a friend that we have done a lot for. And then that person turns around and treat you like a stranger or if they don't owe you.

As human beings that can only give material things to one another. And when those things are not returned to us we get mad. And for some of us the friendship is ended. But not for Jesus even after their abandoning him the first thing he did after being raised from the dead was to seek them out. And after telling them how much he loved them. He later came to them on another day while they had been fishing all day and had caught nothing. He turned around and blessed them with so many fish that they could not even pull in the net. And after that he even prepared the charcoal fire for them and was already cooking fish. So if you think that working and fighting for your salvation is hard. Look at what Jesus had to go through. There has not been before or after a greater sacrifice than this. You would think that the blind man that he gave vision to would at least be there. Or the soldier daughter that he brought back to life would have shown up with his daughter just to show her and say that is the man that saved your life.

The friend of mine that I told you earlier that served ten years in prison and never told on me. I might have written him two times. I watched on television about three months ago a man rob an old lady that was in a wheel chair for her social security check. What kind of people are we? Could this be another reason we all fall short of the glory of God? I think it might also have something to do with the fact that the world is so wicked and selfish and loaded with greed. You had better work and fight for your salvation because we are surely living in the last days. Loneliness is one thing but to die alone is another thing. Who will be there for you? We know from his works and his fighting for our salvation that Jesus will. So we had better beware and fight and work for our salvation. Because it appears that we have very little time left.

Therefore to sum up this chapter we take our faith to activate our works so that our hopes will become our reality. Stop doing the things that are vile and evil. Work to change the bad habits in your life. And if that means getting professional help then get professional help. If you need medication then get and take your medication. Whatever work that you need to do start doing it. And once you have changed the negative and shameful things in your life. Then fight to keep them out of your life. The fighting is continuing to perform the things necessary to remain in your salvation.

Also I would like for you to remember that our fight is not only one of human and fleshly desires. It is also one of higher authorities. Remember Ephesians 6; 12 where the bible says that, 'because we have a wrestling, not against blood and flesh, but against the governments, against the authorities, against the world rulers of this darkness, against the wicked spirit forces in the heavenly places".

Therefore we have to be prepared to not only to watch out for others and ourselves but also for the invisible forces that the devil throws at us that we can't even see. The devil's whole purpose is to keep us from God. I can remember reading and studying my Bible and then someone would come knocking on my door. And it would be someone that had drugs and alcohol. That is how the invisible forces of Satan the Devil works. So watch out for these types of things. Our salvation depends on having accurate knowledge, that's' our next chapter.

CHAPTER SIX

Having Accurate Knowledge

In order for us to receive salvation we need to have the accurate knowledge of God. As I told you earlier in this book that we are damaged goods. And we need to be repaired. We have tried everything that we could possibly think of to rid ourselves of our pain and suffering from whatever it is in our lives that has keep us so unhappy and depressed. And so far nothing has worked.

Therefore we need to go directly to the source of our creation. And since God is our creator we need to go to him. Therefore we need to know who he is, what he is and what he requires from us. This information is in his holy word the Bible. That is why there has been so many Bible quotes throughout this book. Let me start off by giving you an example why we need accurate knowledge.

August of last year I went to my doctor because I was having problems having a bowel movement. He told me that I needed a colonoscopy and we scheduled an appointment to have the procedure done. During the procedure I was in so much pain that I screamed throughout the process. My doctor continued to give me more drugs to ease the pain. When it was over I could barely stand up. The pain was overwhelming it took me twenty minutes just to put my pants back on. On the ride home the pain was terrible I could hardly sit up straight and it also hurt when I sat down.

I called my doctor and explained to him what was going on with me and he told me that it was normal after the procedure. Two to three days later I was still in pain therefore I called his office again. He told me that I had some kind of disease and that he would call in a prescription for me to pick up at my local drug store. The medication that he gave to me did nothing for my pain. I therefore went to the emergency room. They could find nothing wrong and during the next thirty days I had been to the emergency room three times for the pain in my stomach.

To make a long story short after about six months of off and on pain I decided it was time to go to a different doctor. I told him what had happened and what I had been experiencing since that procedure. He asked me the name of the doctor that performed the procedure and I told him. He left me in the patient room and when he came back he said to me. Mr. Clark I hate to tell you this but the doctor that performed the colonoscopy is not licensed or certified to perform that kind of procedure. And that he never should have done it.

Today is August the first 2009 and I am still having problems with my stomach a year later. The point is had I had the accurate knowledge that my doctor was not liscense or certified to perform this type of procedure I would have never let him do it. Therefore I suffer today because of it.

Not having the accurate knowledge of God can cause just as much pain in our lives if not more. The first thing that we need to know about God is that God is love. There is nothing associated to or with God that is not love. So the first thing we need to know that when we have problems in our lives it is not God's fault or his doings. Our problems come from our forefather's disobedience of God. And it is through this source that we grow old and die. It is through this source that we become drug addicts and alcoholics It is through this source that we are gamblers, prostitutes, and killers. Our forefather is the cause of our over eating and our depression and all other sicknesses that we have. Our forefather brought fourth selfishness, our greed and our envy. It was the first man and woman that caused us to become jealous and hateful. It was through them that we are sinners. It is through them that we are fornicators and liars. They are the ones that brought fourth us becoming thieves. They alone are responsible for us being imperfect.

I will not tell you every scripture from the Bible book of Genesis, because I want you to begin to work and fight for your own salvation.

But the things that I have quoted to you can be found in the first two chapters of the Bible book of Genesis.

However, I will share with you this, that in Genesis chapter two verse; six it states "after, that God saw everything he had made and, look! It was very good". So everything that God created was very good. None of his creation had any faults and all were perfect. God gave to man subjection over all that he had created to use as man saw fit. His only rule or law was not to eat from the tree of knowledge of good and evil. God warned our forefather's that if you do disobey me and eat the fruit of this one tree you shall surely die. And what do you think they did? They went ahead and ate from the tree in which God told them not too. This is where our pain and suffering began. And it is still the source of our pain and suffering today.

Because God can not lie, so death was brought forth to all mankind. What comes with death? It is pain and suffering and all the diseases, from small pots to aids. What comes along with death is hate and jealousy, envy and murder? All the things that are not good in this world and in our lives go with death. I will tell you this that hurricanes, tornado's and floods go along with death. All these things came to be because of our forefather's disobedience to God. Drugs, rape, murder and child molestation all go along with our sentence to death, thanks to the first man and woman. I am telling you these things so that when these things come to be you won't blame God. You now have the accurate knowledge of our history and how it came to be.

Our original parents were created in a perfect body and soul. I do want you to know this however. Our original parents did not disobey God immediately. They lived in peace and happiness for sometime. They had subjection to them everything in that garden. So I would assume that they got the big head and decided that they were grown, and could do whatever they wanted to. It's like our own children they love and obey us from birth until 13 to 15 years old. Then they come to the conclusion that they know everything and no longer need your guidance. They become puffed up with doing what they want to. And it is at this point that they struggle with the house rules. They begin to roll their eyes at you and talk smart under their breathe. And for some of us our children tell us want they are not going to do. So for the sake of being honest and using basic common sense let's just say that our forefather's were teenagers when they became disobedient to God. We all know how our teenagers act.

With this understanding in mind you might say why does God allow these things to happen? Let's use my daughter for an example. When she turned 15 years old I started to get the smart talk and the rolling of the eyes. Therefore she left me no choice but to discipline her. And believe me I did. I had made up my mind long before she was born no child of mine would I ever let disrespect me. When she turned 16 years old I sat her down and told her that I have told you what's right and what's wrong. And that I would no longer tell you what to do as much as I use to. Why? It was time for her to start making some of her own decisions. However when she gets to the point that she thinks she is grown then it is time for her to get out of my house and take care of herself.

This is the same way that our original parents treated God. They came to the conclusion that we are grown and can do as we please. Therefore God put them out of his house, the Garden of Eden. God was basically saying the same thing that we tell our children when they no longer what to follow the house rules. And although we still love them and would die for them it is time to let them go. It is time for us as parents to say it's time for you to learn for yourself. And when they come to us after they experience some of the things we told them not to do. They tell us I should have listened when you told me no to do that. And we sometimes say I told you. But, as loving parents we just shake our heads. It truly hurts us as parents to watch our children make mistakes that end up hurting them.

God fells the same way. It truly hurts our lord whom has given us so much undeserved kindness to watch us suffer. But like I said earlier that God can not lie. And he told our parents that if you disobey me then you shall surely die.

So, all of the pain and terrible things in this world is a part of death. God probably cry all day long watching us destroy ourselves. Take this into account. I remember my mother and father telling me to stay off the street coroners because there is nothing good out there. However, I didn't listen and what I found on those coroners was alcohol and drugs. Not to even mention all the crimes I participated in, look at me now. Fifty years later I am suffering from being disobedient. The very things that I picked up on those coroners are the same things that have kept me so unhappy. My disobedience through all of these years brought me to the point of wanting to kill myself. So let us stop blaming God for all of these problems and work and fight for your salvation.

Now because God is love and he loved us so much. He gave us a way out of this mess our original parents got us into. John 3;16 says that "God loved the world so much that he gave his only begotten son. In order that everyone exercising faith in him might not be destroyed, but have everlasting life". Our children go out into the world and make mistakes and we as parents allow them to come back home, if that is what is needed. We do these things for our children and we are not perfect. God being perfect and God is love. How much more than we, do you think he will do for us? Please allow me to explain something to you. What I want to talk to you about is three different ARKS that God gave to allow us to try and save ourselves from ourselves.

ARK ONE ---- Noah's Ark -- the seed of our original parents got so bad in their deeds. God saw that the badness of man was abundant in the earth and every inclination of the thoughts of his heart was only bad all the time. God felt regret that he had made man in the earth, and he felt hurt in his heart. So God said"I am going to wipe men whom I have created off the surface of the ground from man to domestic animal, to moving animals to flying creatures of the heavens, because I do regret that I have made them". Now I want you to understand that God can not lie. So when he told our original parents to be fruit and multiply this had to happen. Therefore God saw the man Noah, who was the only good creature on earth and told him to build an ark that I might save mankind. He further told Noah to take a male and female of every living creature upon the earth with him. God loved the world so much that he saved us through Noah's Ark. God did destroy everything and everyone that was not in that ark. By Noah being the only good man on earth it was God's hope that Noah's off springs would be good too. Keep in mind that God can not lie. Therefore when I talked about God's hope for us, it was through Noah a new generation was born.

ARK TWO---- The Ark In The Tabernacle

God told Moses to build an ark to protect the children of Israel from all types of harm. This ark was to be made out of acacia wood and it was to be overlaid with pure gold inside and outside. It was also to have a molding of pure gold all around it. Inside this ark were three things the two stone tablets with the Ten Commandments written on them. There was also Aaron's staff with the spouted leaves on it. Also inside this ark was a jar of manna. All three of these things represent the saving of lives. The stone tablets with Ten Commandments written on them. Represent what we have to do according to God in order to live and how we should live to keep us from harm. When the Ten Commandments were broken by anyone disobeying God death appeared.

The staff that Aaron had that budded represented that while the children of Israel were in the dessert they complained against Moses and Aaron. Fourteen thousand people die because of their complaining. God told Moses to get 12 staffs one from each one of the twelve tribes of Israel. Put the names of ancestral leaders on them. Put Aaron's name on the tribe of Levi's staff then place them in the tabernacle in front of the Ark of the Covenant, where I will meet you. Buds will spout on the staff of the man I have chosen.

Then I will finally put an end to all this murmuring and complaining against you. This prevented more complaining and more deaths.

The jar of Manna represents the food that God rained down from heaven in order for the children of Israel to eat while in the dessert. All three things inside the Ark saved lives. The ark was inside the tabernacle that was build. This tabernacle was a place where God dwelt in front of the children of Israel. The cloud of the lord rested on the tabernacle during the day, and at night there was a fire in the cloud so all the people of Israel could see it. At that time in history man had to atone for all his sins by sacrifices of animal's blood. And I mean for every type of sin and all sins. This is the same ark that Joshua carried around the city of Jericho for seven days and brought the walls down, so that the children of Israel could over take the city.

ARK THREE----- Jesus Christ

Mankind still continued to disobey God that there was no other way for God to save mankind. Accept by the blood of his first born, Jesus Christ. For God loved man that much. Jesus Christ, represent the saving of life. No longer do man need to sacrifice animal's blood to be forgiven for their sins. When God sent his son to die on the torture stake for us that was the ultimate sacrifice and the last ark to save mankind. Jesus said to "spend your energy seeking the eternal life that I, the son of man, can give you. For God the father has sent me here for that very purpose" (John 6; 27). Also John 3; 35 says "that the father loves his son, and he has given him authority over everything. And all who believe in God's son have everlasting life". We all know the famous Bible verse at John 3;16, where it says that "God so loved the world that he gave his only son,so that whoever believes in him will not perish but have eternal life". God has put so much work into giving us a way to receive salvation.

He has also fought over and over again and again to give us our undeserved salvation. You might be asking yourself, what does this have to do with me ridding myself of my addictions and the reasons for my unhappiness. Have you not been paying attention to what you have been reading? You and I are damaged goods and we are in desperate need of repair. God is the only person that can repair us, but we need to have the accurate knowledge in order to receive those needed repairs. Listen people there are no more comings to receive salvation. Jesus Christ was it. Your happiness depends on your knowledge of Jesus Christ.

I only brought to your attention about the other two arks so that you could be enlighten on how hard God has been working and fighting for your salvation. And if God can extend his self this far for us, we can surely put some work and fight into our own salvation. The reason we have all of our problems from addictions to death is because we don't know God. Listen before I move on to more accurate knowledge. If you had the accurate knowledge from the beginning you would not have become whatever you are that has you so unhappy. With the accurate knowledge you would not do the things that you do that keeps you depressed. With the accurate knowledge you would not be so hateful and full of jealousy.

I tell you that with the accurate knowledge we would have given up our defects and short comings long before Life by Suicide. All have sinned and fall short of God's glory. With the accurate knowledge it is not too late to receive God's undeserved kindness and through that everlasting life. But while we are still living we want to be happy therefore you need to know what to do that can make you happy. And that is having the accurate knowledge of God.

Let me explain to you Life by Suicide. The word Life represents a relationship with God. God he is the giver of life. And we can only live in a happy state of mind, body and soul with a relationship with God. There is no other way. Suicide represents the death of our old self. That self that is so unhappy because we don't know how to live. It's that self that has become so desperate that we need something to make us feel better. Drugs and alcohol, food, gambling. Sex with other's of the same sex, Sex without marriage. We overeat and steal and commit fornication. We do so many different things seeking happiness and peace. The list goes on and on. Yet we never find what we are looking for because we have no idea what will truly make us happy. All of these things make us feel good for a very short period of time and then we have to repeat them to continue in our happiness. Having the accurate knowledge will allow you, or at least give you the opportunity to make a decision to change. God has everything to do with our happiness and our salvation.

I can not give you all the accurate knowledge of God, because I am still learning myself. Every relationship with God is different, that's why they are called personal relationships. To one person he gives wisdom and to another love and yet to someone else the power of prayer. God gives everybody something special in their lives to work with. For some of us it's our voices so that we can praise him and other the power to teach.

I was telling my daughter the other day to get off of the phone and pick up the Bible and read two chapters. She asked me why she had to read the Bible. I told her so that you can form your own relationship with God. She then stated, daddy you already talked to me about God. I told her regardless put the phone down and do as I told you. After she had read the Bible I told her why it is so important that she have her own relationship with God. I explained to her how to form that relationship. I explained it to her in this manner. Your best friend became your best friend from talking and spending time with each other. And by doing things together and believing in the same things. You guys probably even think alike. That is the same effort you have to put into your relationship with God.

In order for you to spend time with God you have to read his word, the Bible. You need to talk with him through your prayers. And you need to know what he expects from you. We have to do the same thing.

Let's move on to more accurate knowledge. Let's talk about the taking of communion. This is what the Bible says about taking communion. "This cup is the covenant between God and you, sealed by the shedding of my blood. Do this in remembrance of me as often as you drink it. For every time you eat this bread and drink this cup, you are announcing the lord's death until he comes. So if anyone eats this bread or drink of this cup of the lord unworthily, that person is guilty of sinning against the body and the blood of the lord. This is why you should examine yourself before eating and drinking from the cup. For if you eat the bread or drink the cup unworthily, not honoring the body of Christ, you are eating and drinking God's judgment upon yourself. That is why some of you are weak and sick and some have even died" 1 Corinthians 11;27-30.

Taking communion is not something to play with or take likely. I read my Bible to find out if Judas took communion with the rest of the disciples. In the book of Matthew, Mark and Luke it appears that he did have supper with them. However he was dismissed before the Lord's Supper, or the taking of communion. John's account talks about Jesus washing their feet. However for the sake of the other three disciples we will assume that Judas did not participated in the Passover meal.

However you do understand what happened after he left the others. After doing what he did the pain and guilt was so dramatic that he was unable to live with his self. Therefore that same night he hung himself, and he didn't even take a part in this special event, he was just there for the evening meal. Also, let's take a look at Peter he did however participate in this special event. And that same night he denied Jesus three different times. It hurt him so bad that the Bible says he ran off and weeped bitterly. Peter knew that he had not only turned his back on Jesus, but also the true son of God. Look at what happened to the remaining disciples they all ran off and left Jesus alone. These were men who saw with their own eyes the things that Jesus had done.

Communion is nothing to play with. If you take communion and you are having sex without being married then you are disrespecting the body and blood of Christ. If you are taking communion and screaming at your husband, wife or children then you are disrespecting the body of Christ. If you are lying you are disrespecting the body and blood of Christ. If you are a drug user or drug dealer and take communion you are disrespecting the body and blood of Christ. If you steal you are disrespecting the body and blood of Christ. I am not just talking about shop lifting. I am talking about any form of stealing and lying to receive money or something of value that you did not honestly work for. That could be lying on your time card at work or cheating the government out of money through social security or unemployment benefits. If you are doing anything that is not in accordance with the teaching of the Bible then you are disrespecting the body and blood of Jesus Christ. The list of things that we should not be doing goes on and on. So if you are participating in any of these things then you better watch yourself.

Because the Bible says that this is why some of you are weak and sick and some have even died. Sickness can be anything between the common flu to aids to cancer. Sickness can be drug and alcohol addictions. Sickness can be overeating to depression. Weak in this Bible verse means that you are not strong enough in your spirit to even help yourself. And even though you pray about things you still can't seem to help yourself and it seems that your prayers are not being answered. Stop taking communion and disrespecting the body and blood of Jesus Christ. No man knows what another man is thinking except that man himself. Therefore examine yourself to see if you are worthy to eat the bread and drink the blood. My only point here is to give you accurate knowledge. Do as you please with

Life By Suicide

the knowledge, just be careful that you are not so weak and sick and eventually die. Let's move on to another topic.

Tithes, the Bible says that God loves a cheerful giver 2 Corinthians 9:7. Now Abraham gave to the king of Salem a tenth of what he received from the war with Kedorlaomer and his allies. That is what Abraham wanted to give from the bottom of his heart. No where does it say that he was required to do that. And since the Bible says that God loves a cheerful giver what Abraham gave was seen as fit in God's eyes.

Abraham did this willingly and full of good spirits. However, no where else have I found the ten percent law. I am not saying that you should or should not give ten percent of your income. What I am trying to say to you that if ten percent is a burden to you then you are not giving it in a cheerful manner. And maybe you should give what you can from your heart. Then at least God will approve of your gift. The Bible states in the book of Exodus chapter 25 that the Lord said to Moses, tell the people of Israel that everyone who wants to may bring me an offering. And in another version of the Bible it says speak to the sons of Israel that they may take up a contribution for me. From every man whose heart incites him you people are to take up the contribution of mine. So you can also see here that God only wants you to give if it is in your heart

You should also understand this that the children of Israel were slaves in Egypt for 430 years and they were not paid for their work. It was through the grace of God that they left Egypt wealthy. God told Moses to tell the children of Israel to go to the Egyptians and asked for want they wanted and God made sure that the Egyptians gave it without any fuss. So, later on when God told Moses to go to the children of Israel and ask the people to build me a tabernacle. It was with the riches that God allowed them to take from Egypt.

Therefore don't be fooled into how much you are suppose to give just make sure whatever you give is with a cheerful heart. And that you want to give what you have given. And not want you can or can't afford to give. This is where the problem comes into play. Who are you giving your tithes to and what organization? Now days a lot of churches are not teaching the Bible and their service is all about money. I went to one of the well know churches in Seattle.

I had never been there before and was greeted at the door. Given a visitor's card to fill out and I sat down. After filling out the card one of the deaconess came and got the visitors card from me. The choir sang two songs and the tray passing began. One of the deacons made an announcement and the tray came again. The choir sang one more song and the tray came again. The preacher came out and gave a sermon full of screaming and jumping up and down. I truly did not understand one word he said.

Before I knew it he was calling out the names on the visitor's card. I knew that I did not want to go up on the stage where the preacher and the other visitor's were. However, the lady that had given me the card when I first came in. Came over to me after saying out loud, I think this is Michael right here. Then the preacher started calling me to join him on the stage. I therefore said that's alright, I'm fine. This guy would not take no for an answer. I finally got up and walked on stage. The preacher started from the first person to the last person, which was me. He asked everybody the same three questions. One did you enjoy the service? Two would you like to become a member of this church? And three are you willing to give a tenth of your earnings to the church. Everybody on stage answered yes to all three questions. Keep in mind that this is a nice size church and congregation.

The preacher now comes to me. And asked me if I enjoyed the service, I responded saying that I could not understand what he was saying. He then asked me if I wanted to join the church, I told him that this was my first time coming to this church and that I did not know at the time. He then asked me if I were to join the church would I be willing to give a tenth of my earnings to the church. I told him no. This man turned towards his congregation and looked directly at me and said get away from me Satan. I stood there in front of three hundred people or more while he was saying things like, I have told you many times that sometimes Satan is among us. Satan sometimes comes to church to disrupt God's people. This is a perfect example of how Satan sends his people to do his dirty work. He then turned back to me and said I dismiss this demon from our church. I looked at him like he was crazy and walked off the stage and headed directly for the door. The looks on the congregations face was amazing. They were all looking at me as though I was a demon or Satan himself. People were actually moving out of my way. As if I would cast a spell on them. I have never enjoyed any service or preaching where the minister is jumping up and down making all kinds of growling sounds. Noises that are not understood by everybody or I should say anybody.

Some people try and say that the minister is speaking in tongues. Well the Bible says that if anyone has the gift of speaking in tongues then he should only speak in tongues when there is an interpreter there to explain what is being said. Otherwise how can the people know what you are saying or even who you are talking too. Tithes in this matter for me would be giving to support the false teachings of Jesus Christ. If, the teachings of Jesus Christ is not being taught then you are giving your tithes to undermine the true accurate knowledge of God. There is no other way to put it. We must remember that Satan is working hard to keep us from our salvation and is using the teachings of Christ to confuse those that do not have the accurate knowledge.

This is why you must read and study the Bible for yourself. Your minister can not give your salvation to you and neither will you receive it through tithes. And you definitely won't receive it if you are supporting the false teaching of Jesus Christ. It is just as many drugs in prison as it is on the streets. And it is so with the church, there are just as many demons and false teachings in the church as it is on the streets. Church is the logical place for Satan to bring forth the false teachings of God's knowledge for us. Listen very carefully here, Satan went to heaven to talk bad about Job to God. Therefore, what would make you think that he will not go to church? Be careful who you are giving your tithes to. You do not want to defeat the purpose in which you are working towards which is your salvation. Also understand this because of all the false teachings know to whom and for what you are tithing. If your tithes are going towards you pastor's third Cadillac and second winter home. Or his one hundredth suite and pair of shoes then maybe you are not being taught the accurate knowledge of God.

In these days and times the giving to the church should be for these reasons. It would be to spread the news about Jesus Christ and his kingdom to come. Also to help those in need of whatever it is that is needed. From the senior citizen who needs extra money for medication, to the family that just lost their jobs and need rent money for the upcoming month! It means using these funds for helping out people in need. That is what Jesus did through out his entire life showing love and compassion to those in need. Rather it was by feeding the hungry or healing the sick. Therefore be full of good spirits when you tithed.

At one point in my life I was working a job in Seattle. Maybe a couple years out of prison and I was trying to stay focused on righteousness. So I was dedicated to my job and walked a mile to work after the bus had dropped me off. And then I would walk a mile back to the bus stop after I had gotten off from work, in which I had to catch two more buses to get home. My total time between the walking and the buses was about five hours to and from work everyday. One day as I was walking while it was snowing this car pulled over and asked me where I was going and if I needed a ride. I still had over a half of mile to walk so I took the ride. On the way to my job this man introduced himself to me and told me that he see me walking everyday. And he always wondered what kind of person I was and that he had thought about giving me a ride many times. But had not done so; because of the dangers of this world, picking up strangers. As we pulled into the parking lot of my employer he stated to me that he had just brought his brand new truck that he was driving and that his wife also had a brand new car. And he was wondering if I would accept their old car as a gift.

Of course I told him are you kidding me you don't even know me. He told me to call him when I got off from work and he would come pick me. All day at work I was dumb founded and in shock and I continued to say to myself, what kind of joke is this guy trying to play on me? Plus this guy was white. Anyway at the end of my day I decided to give him a call because the worse thing that would happen is that I would have to catch the bus anyway. I called him and within 30 minutes he was there at my job. He said your name is Michael, right. I told him yes it is! He said this is what I want to do. Take you to my house and introduce you to my wife, then we will go look at the car in the garage and if you want it you can have it.

Life By Suicide

Now I really can't believe what is going on here. I'm thinking that this guy must be some kind of serial killer or something. However, I knew that I had been on the streets all my life and could handle whatever he thought he was going to do to me. I kept my guards up and paid attention to his every move.

We arrived at his house he went inside and came back out with his wife and introduced us. And from that point we all three went into the garage to look at the car. It was a 1979 Toyota Corolla and it was in great if not mint condition with the original 79 thousand miles on it. The outside of the car did not have one dent in it and the paint job seemed brand new. The inside of the car was clean, not a spot anywhere. This was the year of 1993 so even though the car had age on it you could tell that it had been taken very good care of. He gave me the keys and told me to take it home with me and drive it to work tomorrow and if I want it we will have the title changed tomorrow on our lunch hour.

I did as he said and he never even asked me for my phone number or address, nor did he ask me for identification. I loved that car and on my way to work the next day I stopped at the bank and withdrew five- hundred dollars for him. I called him on my lunch hour and we went and had the car put in my name. I offered him the five hundred dollars and he refused it over and over again. He said that God had blessed him and his wife and that he knew when he seen me walking in the snow that God wanted him to give me that car. So he was just doings God's will and he would only accept a thank you from me. This is tithing with a cheerful heart, as I said.

This next topic is about to make some of you very mad. So, mad that you may stop reading this book. The only thing that I can say about that is it is your salvation at risk and not mine. When I talk about the Bible I always give you the Bible scriptures so that you can see for yourself if I am telling you the truth.

Now let's talk about this belief that when good people die they go to heaven. God placed the seas and oceans where they would best serve his purpose and all that is in them. The trees he placed firmly in the ground so that their roots could provide the food they needed from the earth in order for them to grow. He placed the angels where he wanted them to be. And he also placed mankind exactly where

Michael F. Clark

he wanted them to be, on earth not in heaven. It was never God's intentions for mankind to live in heaven.

Everything that God created was very good and put exactly where he wanted it. Therefore mankind was to live on earth and not in heaven. Everything that mankind needed to survive and stay alive was placed on this earth for him to use as he saw fit. Nothing that mankind needed to live was in heaven, all things for man was upon the earth. Man did not need to go to heaven for water, food or shelter. It was all here on earth for him. Let me say this one more time, there was and is nothing that mankind has ever needed to survive and to care for his daily needs in heaven. It is and has always been on this earth that we met our daily needs.

Also, I would like for you to think about this. When God created mankind we were perfect and in his own image. And God did not want us in heaven then. So you tell me at what point did God change his mind and decided to move us to heaven. Was it after we disobeyed him, or was it after we committed murder and stole from each other. Or was it when we killed his only son, Jesus Christ. I would really like for you to work with me here and tell me. When did God decide to move us to heaven? We have not done one thing right according to God's plan for us. As a matter of fact we have done the very opposite of God's plan for us.

That is one of the reasons that the Bible says that all have sinned and fall short of the glory of God. The Bible says that no one is right. Do you think that God is a fool? Listen when you were perfect and in God's image you were not welcome in heaven. Now that we have done everything that God asked us not to do you have the nerves to think that you are going to heaven. God continued to love us with undeserved kindness and sent us miracle after miracle. To, show us his love and righteousness. God gave us prophet after prophet, king after king, judge after judge and we still did everything that was detestable to God. Then God sent his only son and we killed him.

So you with all of your religious knowledge tell me; when did God decide that mankind should move to heaven with him? You thief and you liar, and you are a murderer. You fornicator and idolaters. All of you homosexuals and child molesters. Even you good Christians that are not sinners today, when did God decide that you are good enough to go to heaven. Us alcoholics and drug addicts, and the gamblers and the over eaters! Give me the knowledge that you have so rightly deserve.

When did God change his royal mind to accommodate us in heaven? Furthermore what have you done to even think about going to heaven? Where and when did you ever deserve that right? Do not confuse God's love with stupidity.

As I told you earlier that God can not lie and that his word must return to him true. Therefore God has allowed us to live on this earth. He sent is son so that whosoever believes in him might have everlasting life. That life of everlasting is not in heaven and it never was. Listen before Satan was Satan he was a leader among angels until he became greedy and jealous, and wanted to be worshiped himself. This angel was created in heaven by God; but yet the moment that this angel disobeyed God he was thrown out of heaven and therefore became Satan the Devil.

So all of you that have believed your whole life that when you die you will be joining Jesus Christ in heaven, I'm sorry to tell you that you will not. Furthermore, what is it that you will be doing in heaven if you were to go? God does not need you to minister to him, he certainly don't need your help. So please tell me what are you going to do while in heaven? Are you going to teach school? Are you going to sale drugs? Or are you going to do social work? Do you think that you are going to heaven to praise God? Or maybe you think that you are going to just lay back and watch soap operas all day long. Maybe you believe that you will work with Jesus. Just what are you going to do while in heaven? We could not even perform the earthly duties that God gave us so what makes you believe that you will now be invited to heaven. I know that this is hard for you to believe but God does not need your help.

In the Bible book of John 3;13 Jesus said that no man has gone to heaven except him that descended from heaven. The very same person that you say you worship and love (Jesus) says that you are not going to heaven. So why don't you believe him. Also again in the same Bible book of John 8; 21- 23 Jesus tells us again that he is going away and where he is going we can not come. He explains that he is not from this world but from heaven and that we can not go with him. He simply tells us that we are of this world, from the realms below.

And yet people continue to believe that if they believe in the name of Jesus Christ that when they die they are going to heaven. Yes, those of us that believe in the name of Jesus will have everlasting life as God promised. But not in heaven, it was never God's intention for us to be in heaven. Why is this so difficult to understand? You think that because Jesus Christ said that in my father's house there are many rooms (John 14; 1-4) that he meant that you will be following him to heaven. No, that is not what he meant and neither was he talking to you. It is a known fact that Jesus Christ taught in several different ways.

One of those ways was in parables and another way was by telling stories and giving examples. He also talked to the crowds of people along with the religious leaders who did not believe in him. Therefore he spoke to them knowing that there ears and hearts would not understand. He then later explained to his disciples what he meant when they were alone. It is my belief that when Jesus spoke of the rooms in his fathers house he was specifically talking to his disciples while they were alone.

The Bible does mention in the book of Revelations of 144,000 people taken from the earth as a special offering to God and the lamb. These are people that have not defiled themselves in any way. They had no falsehood in them, read revelations 14; 1-5. I do not know who these 144,000 people are, because the Bible says that they were without blemish. No man on earth knows who that 144,000 will be. Just know this if you have ever defiled yourself or is not without blemish, then it's not you. However, just for the sake of this conversation I will take one guess as who one of that 144,000 will be. Enoch, the Bible says that he lived three hundred years in close relationship with God throughout his life. Then again in the book of Hebrews 11;5 the Bible says that Enoch was taken by God without seeing death. However, examine yourself, it is not for me to tell you who you are. I do know for a fact that I am not one of that 144,000.

I have told you the truth about people dying and going to heaven if they were good. And that truth is that they are not going to heaven,

Life By Suicide

but instead have everlasting life on earth. God's original plan for us was this purpose. Throughout the book of John Jesus teaches about everlasting life, not dying and going to heaven. No prophet talks about heaven in that sense and neither did the disciples who walked with Jesus teach that people die and go to heaven. Read the book of John for yourself and fight for your own salvation. Just talking about this is becoming exhausting, because if you don't believe the Bible and the teachings of Jesus Christ then I know that you don't believe me. Especially since every church in the world teaches that when you die you go to heaven. And you have all of these well dressed preachers and ministers with their expensive homes and cars. Why would you believe this drug addict? That has never had any training or schooling about the Bible.

Well you think about this! Paul was Saul until Jesus introduced himself to him. And Paul persecuted and killed Jesus Christ disciples and yet he wrote more books of the Bible than anyone else. Yes! That murderer wrote 17 books in the Bible. This shows that God takes the things that are foolish to the world that he might put to shame the wise men. Read 1 Corinthians 1;27-30 for yourself and become knowledgeable about how God works. There is no boasting in me, because I have nothing to boast about. I have asked God to take my life because I did not what to live anymore. I have lived in so much unhappiness and pain in this life I pretended that I was dead. Therefore you may take what you want or take nothing at all.

Life by Suicide is my last attempt for my own salvation. I am just simply trying to save my own life and doing what God has given me to do. As I told you from the very beginning of this book that I am a very unhappy man and wishes that I was dead. So I have no wish to debate with you nor am I looking for your approval. It is my own salvation that I seek and it is through God almighty that his word is being used to seek that salvation. It is either I live a happy rest of my life after Life by Suicide is completed or I simply die.

There are no other choices for me and this I know for a fact. I had no idea that this was going to be a part of this book because I had no idea that this was going to happen to me. Last night I was killed or murderer three times in my sleep. I was first shot in the head twice and then in the second murder I was stabbed in the heart with a butcher knife. And then I was beaten to death with a baseball bat. What I am telling you is that last night August the 21st 2009 I was killed three different ways at three different times in one dream. I woke up after the beating with a baseball bat because I had to use the bathe room. I literally had to use the bathe room because I needed to have a bowl movement. I felt like somebody had beaten the shit out of me, literally. It actually sent me to the toilet. After relieving myself I turned the lights on in my living room and sat down on the sofa wondering what had happened. I was not praying but rather just talking to myself with God. Because I had just been killed three times in my sleep and I was afraid. I certainly was not going to sit in the dark. Plus I believe that people always die around their birthdays and I have a birthday coming up in September. I, asked what was that? And within seconds it was revealed to me that; that was Life by Suicide.

I knew at that moment that some of my old ways had died that night in my sleep. And the dreams are symbolic ways of letting me know that. I immediately started praising God. I knew that my death dreams were me having the opportunity to live. And that my salvation was not at all lost. I knew that God was still allowing me to fight for my salvation. And later on that same day it was revealed to me exactly what each death stood for and meant, praise God almighty. It is not my wish nor is it necessary to explain the meaning of each death. That is my revelation that should be kept to me and maybe those that I believe; believe, it's not for public knowledge. It is however my wish that this God given book help someone other than myself.

I am not seeking fame from this world nor am I seeking fortune from this world. I would hope that my book be published and read by millions of people. But I cannot and will not make stories up and turn the word of God around to make money for myself or to make you feel better. Your feelings are not important and neither is the money involved.

I have lived off of nothing all of my adulthood life. I have stored nothing on this earth for my future or my daughter's future. I am a poor man in earthly goods and desire only happiness. I seek no approval from this world

I am very sick and tired of living. This world has brought to me nothing but pain and suffering. You can have it, it's all yours I just want to do God's will for me and live the rest of my life in some sort of happiness. I want the everlasting life that God intended for me to have. I only want peace and happiness for myself and my daughter. It is God's will that I do what I am doing to get you to understand his true word. I am tired and I am lonely and I am depressed. My wish is to simply work and fight for my salvation so that when God does grant my wish to rest in peace that he won't leave me there. My hope is that God will remember me when the day of resurrection comes. I have no wishes to impress you with my writings or my undeserved kindness in which God has given and shown to me.

My only wish is that I might be able to live after I die. I started writing this book because I was so depressed with my life and wanted to die. God would not allow me to die from my prayers and talks with him. I decided to commit suicide. Then the love for my daughter came to mind and I knew that I could not leave my daughter in this world by herself. With the possibility of her thinking that I killed myself because I didn't love her. Therefore Life by Suicide was born. It was the animal backed in the coroner feeling. I had no other choice; there was no other real alternative for me to live. I was a broken man then. And my fighting and working on my salvation was a selfish one.

It is not my will to include things in this book to change your mind about your beliefs, that's God's doing not mine. It is and has been very hard for me to talk about some of the things that I have. But my life would have not been worth living if I had not followed God's instructions while writing.

I started writing this book on September the 30th 2008 and it is August the 22nd 2009 today. It has taken me close to one year to put this book together; however it took me fifty years to live it. And all of my life I have thanked God and have given him the glory for all that I have been through. I have never, not remembered God regardless of my hate or my pain and suffering. God has always been my driving force to try again and to not give up. I have only told you things that I have lived and not things that I wish for you to believe. I knew from my childhood that God had chosen me to teach his

Michael F. Clark

word but my fears and lack of God fearing undeserved kindness and the ways of this world has held me back. My life has brought me to death and wanting to kill myself. But God would not allow this to happen until his plan for me has been completed, which brings us back to Life by Suicide. During this one year of writing I have been through so much and have experienced more spiritual things that I knew in my mind and heart. But, yet I had not lived them. These experiences are saving my life and I hope that your minds and hearts will come to understand that God loves you to. And that you come to realize that your salvation of everlasting life is worth working and fighting for.

It is time for me to move on to another subject that also will hurt your beliefs. Living in heaven with God was never God's plan for us. Now let's talk about those who do not believe in the name of Jesus Christ and lack the faith in him. These people will not go to a place where they will burn forever and ever. In which you call hell. I will not spend precious time on this subject because it makes no sense and only fools would ever believe that God could be that evil. The Bible says and actually Jesus was doing the talking at this time. Jesus said that the father is in me and I am in the father, if you have seen me then you have seen the father.

After all the things that mankind did to Jesus while he was in human form. Mankind hated the son of God and humiliated him. Then since that was not enough we killed him. The last thing that Jesus Christ said to his father was God forgive them for they know not what they do. Where is the hate and evilness in that comment at the time of death? That statement shows nothing but pure love and compassion. So once again wise and understanding man of God. When did God create or ever say to himself let's send man to a place where they will burn forever and ever? I will tell you this; that you people have no knowledge of God and neither do you honestly seek him. At what point from this great amount of love did this great amount of hate become. Jesus Christ was dying on the cross or stake, whatever you want to call it. After having a crown of thrones placed on his head and watching people gamble for his clothing. After listening to people mock both him and his father, almighty God. After watching all of his disciples run off and leave him alone and after having nails driven through his hands and feet. After being pierced in the side with a spear and being given a sponge of sour wine instead of water. The only thing that our lord and savior could think and feel was to ask his father, God to forgive them, for they know what not they do. You great wise man tell me at what point did God bring the word burning forever and ever into the picture. Do you see how foolish your beliefs sound? What you have been thinking and believing is foolish and stupid.

I was telling my daughter the other day that she gets on my nerves even when she is not here. She said to me; how is that possible. I told her that for one thing when you leave your alarm clock on and it goes off at 5;45 am or 7;00 am and you are at your friends house for the weekend, I have to get out of my bed and turn it off. When you leave your bedroom or the bathe room window open and the wind blow the window blinds all over the room I have to get up and close the window or adjust the blinds so that I won't hear that noise. When you are out in the streets meaning away from home I worry about you. While you are being sixteen years old I worry about you. While you are living your life I worry about you. And it is all due to the fact that I love you.

This is the same thing that God goes through with us. He worries about us, because he loves us and wants us to be safe and happy. I would never think of burning my child forever and ever. How you could think or believe that God would do that to you is unbelievable. Where is your faith? I have found a new respect and honor for Noah and Moses. I can't even imagine what they went through trying to teach the word of God to such ignorant people while being mocked and laughed at. I am not even talking to you, but rather writing to you and you are getting on my nerves.

You are draining me of my energy and strength. And it is all because I know that you have no understanding of what I'm talking about. And even if you do you refuse to change your belief because this is what you have believed all of your lives. However, it is God's wish for me to tell you these things and not mine, therefore you have been told. Jesus Christ said that his sheep will hear his voice and would come to him, so if this is foreign to you and you do not understand, so be it.

Michael F. Clark

However it is 4;17 in the morning and I am tired so I'm going to bed. We will talk more in the morning or should I say when I wake up, because it is already in the morning. One day later I have returned to my writings of Life by Suicide, it has been 24 hours.

Sometimes people believe what they were raised to believe and never venture out on their own to find out if what mom and dad said was fact or not. I was once in a correctional facility and had just arrived there and for the first thirty days I was in orientation; if that's what you want to call it. However, my cell mate was a man named Eric.

Now Eric was in prison for 13 counts of child molestation, all little boys. I hated and could not stand the sight of this man. But I had to sleep in the same cell with him for thirty days. I had already asked the guards to move either him or me but they refused to saying that the prison was full and there was no other place for either one of us. I told Eric not to say one word to me while we were bunking together. Now Eric was no small man but he was weak in constitution and in will. Therefore we stayed in our cell 23 hours a day for two weeks without ever speaking one word to each other. I then decided to ask him what made you rape all of them little boys and why.

At first he didn't want to talk about it but finally he did. And what he told me is that he thought that it was normal because as long as he could remember his father and grandfather were having sex with him. He stated that his uncles and the other men in the family were all having sex with the kids. From his childhood to adulthood he was having sex with grown men. And once he was grown he started having sex with little boys. Of course that was a reason but to me it was no excuse. However we talked about it a little every day and he told me more and more about his illness. I really came to believe that in the beginning he really was a victim; in which he was. But as a grown man he should have known better and he agreed with me. He told me that by the time he realized what he was doing was wrong he had learned to enjoy it and that it had become a need to him.

After I was moved to my own cell and would see Eric off and on we would still talk. However I took a lot of crap from some of the other inmates because of that. A child molester is the most hated and picked on inmates in prison. Eric did receive help for his problems and rather or not he has changed I do not know. The point to that story is just because our parents believe in something that does not make it right. And some of us have never read or took time out of our own lives to see if the Bible says what our parents taught us. Therefore we live our parent's beliefs in our adult lives not knowing for our selves, rather it is true or not. As I told you earlier your salvation is in your hands. Neither, preacher or parent will give you salvation. And neither will anyone be able to say to the lord that is what I was taught to believe.

I have told you what I know to be the truth it is totally up to you to do what you choose to do with it. It makes no sense that God would send his children to a place where they would burn forever and ever, that's just evil. Some of our children have done some things to us that hurt really bad. Would you who don't know how to love send your child to a place where they would burn forever? No! You would not and neither would God who knows how to love. The Bible says that God is love. Tell me where is the love in such an evil act? Yes! God has punished mankind for being disobedient but never has he punished us forever and ever. The children of Israel walked in the dessert for forty years as punishment and some even died by the hand of God. But none of them were punished forever and ever.

I remember about a year ago my daughter wanted to spend the night over one of her friend's house. I told her that she could not because it was a school night. She asked me later that day and my answer was still the same. She then called me from school the next day and asked me again. However by now I had become suspicious of her intentions and where and what she really was trying to do. She then had one of her friends call me to tell me that there was no school on Friday. I told my daughter to bring her self home when school was out. Little did she know I had the school's principle's phone number in my personal phone book! So, I called him and he told me that there was school on Friday and that they must be up to something else.

Therefore I called my daughter and told her that she had better bring herself home from school and that I had talked to the principle and he said that there was school on Friday. I called my daughter shortly after the time she should have been home from school to see where she was at. She told me that she didn't know that she had to come straight home and that she was at a friend's house. Now I am really mad because I know she knew better and all the lies over a two day period. Even having her friend's call and lie to me for her.

Now this is Thursday night she calls me and tells me that she does not have a way home and that it is to late for her to catch the city bus. I am livid because this child has been lying to me for days now. I have already decided that either she was about to experience sex or something that she knew she has no business doing. Something was up because she has never lied to me like that and in that fashion and for so many days. However I had no choice but to let her spend the night over her friend's house, because it was too late to catch the bus and I had no other way to go and get her.

Also the person's house that she was at went to the same school as she did and the school bus would pick them up and take them to school. At this point I told her Thursday night that she had better be at school and on time Friday morning. And I also told her to call me as soon as she got to school. Well Friday morning she calls me from the school at 7;15am to let me know that she was at school. I made sure that she was calling from school by looking at my caller I.D screen.

About one hour later the principle called me to ask why my daughter was not in school. I told him that she is in school and that she had just called me from school about an hour ago. He said OK let me go check and find out, because I know that I told you there was school Friday. And it sounded to me that her and her friends was up to some thing. The principle called me back and said, Mr. Clark your daughter did come to school and she used the telephone and left. Now I am so disappointed and mad with her that I already knew this was not going to be punishment with words and property this called for physical discipline. Later on that day when school was out she called to let me know she was on her way home. I told her that I knew that she had not been to school and that she had been lying all week and that she was in serious trouble when she came home. She told me that she was not coming home then and hung up the telephone in my face. And she would not answer her phone when I called back.

Therefore I called the police and reported her as a runaway. The police took a report and told me to call after she had been missing for twenty- four hours. However my daughter called me to let me know that she was safe and told me where she was at. I told her that I had already called the police and reported you as a runaway, so keep running. I later called the police back and told them where she was and that she refused to come home.

The police told me that since I knew where she was she was no longer considered a runaway. However I have been in these streets all of my life by myself so I knew that she had to come home sooner or later. The lady's house that she was at I had met more than once and this situation was one I had experienced more than once. Not my child running away but women falling in love with my daughter and not wanting to return her. Some how my child turned out to be sweet and honorable. And extremely lovable, so women would realize that I was a single father and take it upon them self that I needed their help and my daughter needed a mother. Like I said I've been in this world to long by myself and I knew she would have to come home for clothing or something sooner than later. Therefore I waited it out and just like I knew the phone calls started to come about clothing. I am to hard core for that so I told her that she did not have any clothes here that when you ran away you left those things here and that they belong to me now. And furthermore you were grown enough to run away be grown enough to come and get your clothing. I told her that I was not going to send her clothing to her by somebody else and nobody could come and pick them up for her. Anyway this went on for about a week or more.

My daughter decided that she would go to some of my friends that were professional counselors and social worker's. Therefore she went to them and told them that I was using drugs everyday and drinking so much alcohol everyday that she was afraid for her life and was scared to come home.

Rather she knew or not these people were mandated by law to report any kind of neglect or abuse. Therefore they had no choice but to call the police and child protection services. However, they did call me and tell me what was happening and if I wanted to I could come to their place of business and talk with the police and child services. I went up there but refused to talk with anybody, my intentions were to slap my daughter. They had her hid some where else in the building or office. So I left and they called me and said that the police and child protection worker said that my daughter could stay at her friend's house until they had a chance to talk with me. And they were wondering if she could come home and get her clothing. My answer to that was the same as it was before. I didn't allow her to come and get her clothes until about a week later.

And that was because I still loved my child and I knew she needed her clothing and things. But it was also I was beginning to like having my home to myself without having to clean up behind her and telling her to do this or do that. At one point she called me and told me that she was ready to come home and I told her that I am not ready for you to come home. I told her to stay where she was for another two weeks. That way you will know what it is like to be away from your own home. I explained to her that there is no place like home and that I wanted her to learn that right now. So that the next time you feel like doing what you want to you will know that home is not the place to leave.

I did later have to meet with the child protection worker and I was drinking when she came over. She said to me don't you think it is too early in the morning to be drinking. I told her maybe it is for you but it is not too early for me. However, after their investigation and interview they decided that there was no case and that I had done nothing wrong. My relationship with my friends was damaged and I didn't know if it would ever be repaired.

Eventually I allowed my daughter to come home. But I had never been so badly hurt in my life. My feelings were that my own child had called the police and child protection on me because she wanted to do something that I told her she couldn't. And for a while I fell out of love with my child. I never stopped loving her, but some of the things I used to be willing to do for her I was no longer willing to do. Things like if there was only enough detergent to wash my clothes I use to make sure her clothes were clean before I used what detergent was left. I didn't feel like that anymore and I used to have her dinner ready five times a week; but not anymore. My point to this story is that I would not send my daughter to a place where she would burn forever and ever. There were nights that I cried about what she had done to me.

God would not send his children to a place for them to burn forever and ever just because they did something he told them not to do. God is love and I am talking about pure love. There is no reason to believe that God would do such a thing. Because the Bible says that the foolishness of God is wiser than man, and the weakness of God is stronger than man, 1 Corinthians 1;25. Therefore know that the love of God is more powerful than the love of man.

While living in Seattle there was a man that I grew up with and he lived with my family for some time. He was not any kin to me but my family referred to him as family, therefore I will use the term brother. My brother and I were leaving Seattle to go to Minneapolis. His wife had pasted from an over dose of drugs and he was in a really bad space and place. Somehow I convinced him to come back to Minneapolis with me. We therefore brought our one way bus tickets from Seattle to Minneapolis. You need to keep in mind that we are talking about two drug addicts and alcoholics that had been using for days without stopping. Anyway we are at the bus station waiting for our bus to come and we realize that we had at least another hour before its arrival. Therefore we decide to go outside and find a place to take a hit of crack cocaine. We found a local bar which was about one block from the bus station. We went in, order some drinks and took turns going in the bathe room to smoke crack.

My brother decided that we did not have enough crack to last us from Seattle to Minneapolis and that he was going to jump in a taxi and go get some drugs before the bus came. Well that was not want I wanted to do and so I did not go with him. However, I decided that I could not leave him there in Seattle under the circumstances and the space that he was in. Therefore I got in a taxi and went looking for him. I knew that he would go to the nearest place which was downtown Seattle. I found him and told him to come on but he refused basically because he had not found what he was looking for. We end up going our separate ways. I finally got on the bus leaving Seattle going to Minneapolis without him. It truly bothered me that I had to leave him, but I knew because I am a drug addict that he was not going anywhere in the mind space that he was in. Therefore I had no choice but to leave him. And the main reason being was that my daughter was in Minneapolis and I had to get back.

After arriving in Minneapolis I called my brother's mother in law and asked her had she heard from him. She told me that he called and said that he was in jail and had been charged with murder. Apparently from my understanding someone sold him some bad drugs and would not give him his money back. So my brother killed them. My brother had left home at a very young age and was in Vietnam fighting at the age of sixteen and had become a member of Special Forces. He knew how to kill. My brother went to prison for murder and I went to Minneapolis. Or should I say that my brother went to heaven and I went to hell.

He found God while in prison and became a born again Christian. And I went to Minneapolis to continue in my pain and suffering. He was at more peace in prison than I was living on the streets. As I told you before sometimes being arrested is also being rescued. He was rescued and I continued to live in my dark world of addiction. I remember a letter that I had wrote to him saying that I bet you wish you had brought your butt with me. When I received his letter back he stated that he was glad to be where he was and that God had saved his life and that he hopes and prays that I find a way out of my sickness.

My brother has been released from prison and from what I heard from my sister he is doing really good, praise God. In so many ways God blessed him more than he did me. He was allowed to sit down and focus on what is really meaningful in his life. He was given the opportunity to change while being in an environment that left no room but change or return. While I was given my freedom and my will, I didn't change. His prison turned out to be his heaven and my freedom turned out to be my hell. I have told you before and I will tell you again, that there is a lot of things worst than death in this world. I will tell you that for his eight years in prison he has brought his own home now, has a positive relationship with God and is thinking about getting married again.

My last eight years has been of pain and suffering from the dark and powerful world of drugs. My last eight years has been full of tears

Life By Suicide

and thoughts of suicide. Between my brother and me, who really got the better deal?

However, God has shown his undeserved kindness to both of us. He has given us another chance for salvation and to enter into his kingdom to come. God disciplines those whom he loves and both of us were. God works in mysterious ways and the understanding of his workings are not always understood by mankind. The Bible says in the book of Romans chapter two verses three and four "do you think that God will judge and condemn others for doing them and not judge you when you do them. Don't you realize how kind, tolerant, and patient God is with you? Or don't you care? Can't you see how kind he has been in giving you time to turn from your sins"? Therefore I thank God for the time he has given to my brother and me. Neither one of us will burn forever and ever.

As I continue with Life by Suicide it occurred to me that all you have heard about me is the undeserved kindness that God has shown to me. You have heard of all sorts of criminal activity and drug and alcohol behaviors. I feel like it would be unfair to the readers and to Life by Suicide along with the accurate knowledge if you did not hear about the good man underneath these behaviors. One of the reasons I have not talked about Michael as the original man. Is because; Life by Suicide's purpose is to rid me of all the vile and horrible things in my life. That has kept me from my salvation and from any state of happiness. It was never about the good in me. However, it would be very misleading to the reader if you did not get the full picture of this tortured soul. So as I spend very little time on my good, understand that it is not to boast. But it is only to give you the accurate knowledge of Life by Suicide.

I have always helped anybody throughout my life. Rather that person was eating out of a garbage can or standing on the coroner with their hands out needing money. I have never cared what they might use the money for even though I had some idea. That it might go towards their next bottle of liquor and at the same time they would get them something to eat. I have brought so many different strangers to my home to feed and give a place to live. I have also allowed strangers to come to my home so that they could take a bath and wash their clothing. I have been unemployed and on welfare and taken some of my food stamps. Went to the store and brought food and given it to the local food shelve. I have spread God's knowledge to people and strangers all of my life. As I told you earlier I have loved God from the beginning of my life. Yes! I have struggled doing his will but the love has never failed. One of the things very important to me was that I knew who I loved. There was only one way for me to get to know God. And that was to study the Bible and pray for understanding of his will for me. I did not want to love a God that I had been told about and believe only what I heard. It was necessary for me to learn about him myself.

I remember going to Bible studies with my brother's and sister's and thinking to myself who is this person that wants to burn me forever and ever. Who is this God that gave his only child so that I could live? I remember saying to myself that some of what this preacher is saying makes no sense. How could somebody love me so much that they would let their only child die for me? And that same person hate me so much that if I did something that he did not like he would make me burn forever and ever. I remember saying to myself either this God is a fake or this preacher is lying. Therefore I sought out the truth for myself. And even before my parents changed religions I had my own thoughts and questions about God. Because I was not happy with the explanations and teachings I was hearing from this Bible teacher.

So I have not always done terrible things in my life. I have also done a lot of good things and helped a lot of people. Even in active addiction I was able to help people and did it with joy. My mother and daughter used to always ask me, why do you keep bringing these strange people into your home? My answer was always the same that I could not help it. It is in my blood to help those that need it when I can. The thing that I could not understand was how could some body walk right pass someone eating out of a garbage can and not help them. I could not understand how a person could tell someone no, when asked for help. It is not hard to see that somebody is in dire need. Jesus whole and entire life here on earth was spent helping people. To me if you can't help your fellow citizen what purpose do you serve?

It is God's will for us to love one another. So believe me that my life has not been just one of wrong doings. I have had my good moments throughout my life. As I said earlier in this book it is not about my good but rather the need to rid myself of the wrong in me. So let's move on for I can not and neither is there room for me to boast about any good that I have done. All things were done by God I was just a tool used. I am just becoming the man I truly am. In the Bible book of Ephesians chapter five in verses one and two the Bible says" follow God's example in everything you do, because you are his dear children. Live a life filled with love for others, following the example of Christ, who loved you and gave himself as a sacrifice to take away your sins. And God was pleased, because that sacrifice was like sweet perfume to him"

My quest for my own happiness has not stopped me from helping and loving others. To go along with that is one of my favorite Bible verses, "don't forget to show hospitality to strangers, for some who have done this have entertain angels without even realizing it", Hebrews 13;2. Now let's move on to the next chapter.

CHAPTER SEVEN
Who Am I Today

This chapter is about the, us in ourselves. This means that there are more of us living in this one body than we think. For me there is the drug addict Michael. There is also the alcoholic Michael. I also have the depressed Michael and the Post Traumatic Stress Disorder Michael. And then there is the Agoraphobic Michael. There is also the fleshly Michael. And last but certainly not least there is the Godly Michael. All of these different Michael's have their own personalities and their own thought process. They all have their own behaviors and their own hopes and wishes. They all wish for the fleshly Michael to do their will.

When I went to treatment this last time one of the very first things that came out of my mouth was that I need more than one chair while in group. So that I could have the other me's sit down too. I knew that, because these other people had been living inside of me and that they also needed counseling. They were all a part of the problem. I was being pulled by every last one of them. And I never knew which one of these people would show up or when they would show up. All that I knew is that they were there. The addict Michael wanted me to use drugs. And it reminded me of the good times I would have while using drugs. It reminded me of the good and great sex involved. However it never brought up the horrors or the negative things drugs caused. The alcoholic Michael wanted me to feed it by drinking and it also reminded me of all the fun involved in its use. It also never talked or reminded me of all the pain and suffering involved with its use. Things like not remembering what I had done or even where I had been. It also never reminded me about the hang overs. It never reminded me of all the bad things that I would do and say to people while under its influence. Never did it remind me of how terrible I would feel the next day in my health and in my mind.

Then there is the depressed Michael, the one that saw nothing good in himself. The one that said to me all the time, that you are worthless. This depressed Michael would tell me that nobody in this world loves you nor do they care about you. That is why you have been by yourself for so long. This Michael would say to me that there is no reason for you to get out of bed the people and the world does not need you nor do they want to be bothered with you. You are only good for one thing and that is, nothing.

My depressed Michael would live with me inside its dark and unmotivated world of blackness. It would leave me hopeless and helpless. My depressed Michael is one of powerful sources. It would defeat me before I was even out of bed. Depressed Michael could go to sleep with me and have the power to wake up with me. Its boundries were and still are unlimited. It is capable of bringing forth the other Michael's and controlling them to the point that they follow its desire. And then there was and still is the Post Traumatic Stress Disorder Michael. And his twin brother the Agoraphobic Michael, God, please forbid that they wake up with me together, especially at the same time. They would remind me of all the tragic things that I have been through and saw. Things like seeing my baby sister on the coroner's table with the top of her head completely cut off. And a large Y shape deep cut throughout her chest and stomach. Other things like watching my best friend dying from cancer. And watching her slowly deteriate until death.

You also have the fleshly Michael that desire the ways of the world. It desires the very things that defile me and cause my own unhappiness. This Michael seems to want to battle and do business with all of the other Michael's. It seems to have the desire to want to be in control. And last but certainly not least you have the Godly Michael, the Michael that is underneath, that only wants to please God. It wishes for happiness and to help others. This Michael has a strong and powerful love for God; but at the same time it appears to not have a wholesome fear of God. This Michael is always lurking in the front and yet it is always in the background. This Michael is stronger than any other Michael and yet it is the weaker one. It allows me to believe and to continue to work and fight for my salvation. And yet it bows down to the other Michael's. I am now realizing that this is all due to my strong love for God but yet not having a wholesome fear of God. This Michael is the one that created Life by Suicide. This is the good in me. This Michael has to fight all the other Michael's sometimes one at a time. But most of the time it has to fight all of them at the same time. This Michael is very strong and yet it is very weak.

It is strong because of all the responsibilities it has of maintaining my healthy love for God. And it is strong because it is always fighting by itself. The other Michael's are never the Godly Michael's allied. But the addict Michael will ally with the alcoholic Michael. Or the depressed Michael will be friends with the Post Traumatic Stress Disorder Michael. And they will join forces with the addictive Michael. Even the fleshly Michael will connect with the other Michael's. But never does the Godly Michael have help and cooperation from the other Michael's. And that is why this Michael is the stronger one and yet it is the weaker one. This Michael is always fighting alone against multiple Michael's. All of the other Michael's hate this one Michael. They do not want him to win and they have nothing in common with this Michael.

The other Michael's are associated with the darkness of this world and keeping me from the love of God. It is this one Michael alone that is associated with the light. This Michael wants me to seek happiness and salvation. It is this Michael that allows me to have hope. It is this Michael that I want to be. But as I told you earlier that the things I want to do, I don't do. But the things I don't want to do, I do. These are the people responsible for my actions and reactions. All of these Michael's wants to be medicated and to be present at all times.

Before I went to treatment this last time I was in my back yard drinking alcohol with a friend of mine. However she got so greedy she started to smoke all the cigarettes and began hiding them in her purse. She was also trying to put beers in her purse. I had told her once that she did not have to do that. And I would not have brought the liquor and invited her to my house if I was not going to share with her. So I told her to please stop stealing cigarettes and beers. She continued to do it and I got mad and told her that she could have all of it. Therefore I left her in my back yard by herself. Normally I would have not given her or anybody else my alcohol. However, I had money in my pockets and drugs that I wanted to use, I had planned on using these drugs with her but she got on my nerves with her stealing. I left her and went to my home to use the drugs I had in my pocket.

After about twenty minutes I looked out my back door and she was still sitting out there, talking to herself. Today I realized that she was not talking to herself. She was talking to the other hers. The other people living inside of her, she was doing her best to get them under control. So that she could remain in some kind of decent control before they took over. These other personalities as I told you have a mind and thought process of their own. And after living with and in you for so long they become you, or at least a part of you. They have an active force in your life. Therefore you can not deny them or ignore them for that same reason; they are a part of you. We have fed those other us for so long that they now are living beings.

Society believes that we are people with serious mental illnesses and that maybe true. But it is not just the drug addict and alcoholic who have these other people living inside of them. It is also those in which we call and I quote the normal people as well. It is also the gambler and the over eaters. We all have these other personalities lurking in our souls. For some of us they are not a problem because they are only thoughts because they have not been activated. But for the addict of any sort the activation of these personalities has already begun. If you are doing anything that you do not want to do. But yet you keep doing it regardless of the pain and discomfort that it cause you then there is another you living inside of you. Rather you recognize it or not and rather you believe it or not. These other people are real to the person experiencing them. It is actually not that difficult to understand when you look at the behaviors of someone that suffers. You should also know that these personalities that I refer to as the other yous or other people. They have all been created by us due to our sinful ways. So it does not seem that far fetched when you really think about it. And from whatever point you start from

Life By Suicide

it all goes back to sin in our lives and being separated from God. It all boils down to being unhappy and not being fulfilled. As I told you before that sin is in all phases of our lives and can appear in all kinds of forms.

All of these Michael's were created and born from my own sinful ways and my disobedience to God. If you look at the alcoholic and drug addict Michael, it is not hard to figure out what caused that. What might be a little harder is why was I so unhappy and dissatisfied with myself that I needed a chemical to make me feel better. Life by Suicide has been explaining this throughout this book. The depressed Michael is the son of the drug addict and the alcoholic. Therefore when you throw in his siblings, Agoraphobic and Post Traumatic Stress Disorder Michael you have me. All of these other mes were created by me. I, impregnated myself with them and then gave birth to them. And for thirty years I have been feeding them and raising them as though they were my very own children. These other Michael's began to grow and at the moment they became teenager's they got out of control. And would no longer do as I said, but they did what they wanted to do. They begun to take on a life of their own and make their own decisions. The only problem was that I could not put them out of my house. I was the house. Therefore they became grown men living inside of me. This is the title of this chapter, Who Am I Today?

And therefore once again I need to go back to my creator, God to seek his forgiveness in order for me to rid myself of these men in me. It is as the Bible book of Romans chapter 7; 18-25 says "I know that I am rotten through and through so far as my old sinful nature is concerned. No matter which way I turn. I can't make myself do right. I want to, but I can't. When I want to do good I don't. And when I try not to do wrong, I do it anyway. But if I am doing want I don't want to do, I am not really the one doing it; the sin within me is doing it. It seems to be a fact of life that when I want to do what is right, I inevitably do what is wrong. I love God's law with all my heart. But there is another law at work within me that is at war with my mind. This law wins the fight and makes me a slave to the sin that is still within me. Oh! What a miserable person I am! Who will free me from this life that is dominated by sin? Thank God! The answer is Jesus Christ our lord. So you see how it is; in my mind I really want to obey God's laws, but because of my sinful nature I am a slave to sin". The Bible put it in the most understanding words than I ever could. But that is exactly how I feel. Therefore I wrote word for word that quote from the Bible. Making it a little easier for you to seek your salvation, however you should read it for yourself.

As I told you before in this book that there is no other name in which mankind can be saved from himself and his sinful nature except through Jesus Christ. There is no one else, period. Not on this earth before us nor, on this earth after us. Not in the heavens before us, and not in the heavens after us. The only name for salvation is the name of Jesus Christ. Life by Suicide is my confessions to my God in order for me to receive salvation. It is my way of killing off all the things that defile me. Everything! No matter how embarrassing or shameful. My only hope and chance for this salvation is to kill myself. I am looking forward to my death through Life by Suicide.

The men in me may not like what I am doing. However they are not the ones in power as of this moment. It is going on a full year since I first started writing and those men have surfaced in the past and they have slowed me down. But the Godly Michael would not give up. He just kept fighting and working for my salvation. It is like I said he is the stronger one of them all. This Michael reminds me that nothing can keep me from the love of God. And therefore I keep on trying. I once heard that saints are those who did not give up, but continued the race through all the hard times and finished the race in pure form. They finished the race in tact with all of their beliefs. They fought through every obstacle in the way. They kept their eyes on the prize at the finish line. And they refused to let outside issues distract them from their mission.

I remember when I was a lot younger when I had the constitution to fight for what I believed in. And I would not let go until I received what I thought was due to me. I had this burning desire to win at all cost. However that was before my other Michael's were fully grown. They seem to have taken more than just my testosterone. It appears that they have also stripped me of my will to fight for what I believed in.

For an example when my daughter was born I was thirty four years old. And this was my first child. The mother and I were already having problems so by the time my daughter was born our relationship was almost over. Anyway for some reason or another, my daughter's mother felt like she should have custody of our child. However, she had already relapsed and was in no shape to take care of our child. Not only that, she had done some other things that I was not happy about. It was in my blood that I was not going to let this woman have my daughter. So the fight for custody began. This woman and her attorney's just lied and lied in court over and over. Lies from I physically abused my daughter to sexual abuse. I mean every time I turned around there were new accusations of negative behaviors on my part. This was possible because I had already been to prison three times for assault and arm robberies. So convincing a judge of these charges was not that difficult.

However the family court mediator was a lot wiser than the judge. Then on top of that my daughter's family on her mother's side also lied for my daughter's mother. This made it very difficult for me. Plus at this particular time in history it was very hard for men to get custody of their children. But I refused to give up regardless of everybody telling me to just let it go. And be happy with visitation rights. This did not sit well with me. My feelings then and my feelings now is that nobody is going to dictate to me when and when I can not see my child. This is one of those things that I hate about men who allow women to tell them when they can see their children. I mean it literally burns me up when men let women treat them in that manner. Anyway I kept fighting and fighting and finally got custody of my child. She has been in my custody for sixteen years and will be turning seventeen this November.

However some where along the lines of my addiction I have lost the will to fight. Life by Suicide is a fight for my life. It is an attempt to rid myself of me. It is an opportunity for me to reconcile with my God. The other men in me have distracted me for over thirty years and have kept me from any sort of happiness. As long as I don't fight for me I will remain a slave to weaknesses and sicknesses. Courage is the by pass that cowards need to know.

Today I have found some level of courage to go back to God. I am taking my life back from myself and I am going to live a good and healthy life. As I said in the beginning of this book that by the time I finish writing this book I would be dead. All the information in this book is the poison that is needed to kill myself. I can no longer live with all of these other people inside my body and mind. What I can say is that out of all the pain and suffering that I have been through has made me seek salvation. For I know that my life is worthless without it. I would not seek salvation if I were a happy man. Because I would be happy in this world, but since my pain has brought nothing but unhappiness, I seek out salvation. Happy people don't know that they need salvation, because everything is going well for them. It is only through our pain that we seek change. And through this change we look for help. And after all the false things in this world that we have tried, none of them has helped us. We finally realize that there is only one way out and that is through our salvation. So our pain is not left without reward. We grow up and seek happiness before we die. And it is through this salvation that we live, Life by Suicide.

The Bible says in the book of 2 Corinthians 7; 10 "God can use sorrow in our lives to help us turn away from sin and seek salvation. We can never regret that kind of sorrow. But sorrow without repentance is the kind that leads to death". Therefore I repent and seek my salvation from Michael so that Michael can live.

The Godly Michael has out lived the other Michael's and has allowed me to make restitution for my sins. What more can I say about who I have been and who I want to become. It is all a matter of changing things that have not been good for me and killing them. The more I use the word kill I realize that there is a Michael that was never born. Living the kind of life that I have I am so glad that my Michael demons have never killed another human being. I do know that I have wanted to kill before but my love for God and the knowledge of his word has not allowed me to do it. Actually two times this year I wanted to kill somebody. And yet I did not, because my prayer's has always sustained me. I know that the very best thing for me to do is to pray for my enemies and that is worst than death for them. Therefore I have never had to give birth to that Michael. And I praise God for that.

It is now 3;38 am August the 29th and I have just been awaken out of my sleep from another death dream. These dreams are coming more often than I would have hoped for. However, I do believe that my demonic Michael's are being murderer in these dreams, so it's not that bad once I wake up. But the dreams themselves are frighting. And once again I had to use the bathroom for a bowel moment (it scared the shit out of me) it woke me up. This dream was as clear to me as daylight. I clearly remember a friend and I were drinking and the next thing I knew we were in the wilderness. As we were walking a wild animal that appeared to be some kind of antelope or wild boar started running at full speed towards us. Therefore we took off running, however this thing had four legs and we only had two. It was gaining ground on us fast.

Some how in this dream my friend disappeared in mid air and at that very moment this animal was headed directly for me. At the moment of impact my breathe left my body, but at the moment of loosing my breathe I woke up. I both seen and felt the impact and yet at that very same moment I woke up. I do know the significance to this dream and it does deal with death. Hopefully it is the Life by Suicide death and not my literal death. With my previous dreams I knew it was Life by Suicide dying. But with this dream I am unable to tell the difference. I have always loved my dreams because I believe they are trying to tell me something. So I have always studied my dreams and ask God for help with understanding them. The one thing that I will say is that the friend in this dream has been dead for at least five years now, that's one reason I can associate this meaning with death. Also when he just clearly disappeared in thin air that represented his death and that he was already gone. The moment he disappeared was at the very same moment of impact for me. There is meaning there and I know that the true meaning will be revealed to me later, it always is.

I do not want anyone to misunderstand the other people that might be within us. Because some of these people we have certainly created ourselves. Therefore we have the same right to kill them.

Michael F. Clark

And they must be killed in order for us to have any opportunity to seek salvation.

Today is a very sad day for America at least it is for those of us who understand. I have taken off from writing for the last three hours to pay my respects to Senator Ted Kennedy. And respect and honor is definitely what he deserve, this man dedicated his life to the salvation of others from health care, to helping the poor as well as civil rights. If there was ever a pioneer in our life and time he was it. From the very beginning of this book I have asked for God's guidance in all that it contains. And I feel no discomfort with my God by saying what I am saying concerning this man and his family. The Kennedy's are to America as King David was to Judah and Israel. When you think of the United States of America, you also first think of the Kennedy family. It is as if they were born for this purpose to care for America, They have done it well, very well.

And as a Black man I know that Abraham Lincoln might have freed the slaves, but it was the Kennedy's who let us go. There might always be another first family of the United States of America, but there will never be another royal family of the United States of America. I will tell you something else God is calling his people home. I know you have no idea what I mean by home in this sense but now is not the time to explain. I just wanted to take the time out to recognize this good and great man. May Almighty God bless his soul and may Senator Ted Kennedy rest in peace.

There is one other thing about the Godly Michael he has always been able to recognize things in a different light than most people. For an example I realize that my faith in God can be or may be just as strong as the men God has chosen to do his will. I have never in my life thought that Moses or Abraham was any better than me. I have never believed that King David was more loved by God than me. I believe exactly what the Bible says, and that is, no one is good and all men fall short of the glory of God. I believe that we must all stand before Christ to be judged. And that we will all receive whatever we deserve for the evil or right we have done in these bodies. This Godly Michael believes that he is just as good as the other men God has used and that they are no different from me. They never used drugs. I have never killed anyone. This Michael believes that we all

Life By Suicide

come from the same blood line. And that God is my father too and loves me just as much as he does them.

This Michael also believes that God has used him in ways as well. It may have not been on the grand scale of things as these men and others were. However big or small God has used me to. This book will help a lot of people in these last days. Life by Suicide has been written and published to save myself and those seeking salvation that have not been able to get it from the normal sources. Life by Suicide does not teach or say anything different from what is taught in the Bible. Therefore God might be using me again. Who are you to judge? My Godly Michael believes in God with all of his heart, mind, body and soul. I don't want to talk too much about this because it will take away from an upcoming chapter. I will tell you this that Paul had committed some very serious crimes against the lord including murder. And yet God found favor in Paul and gave to him power to do unusual miracles, so that even when handkerchiefs or cloth that had touched his skin were placed on sick people, they were healed of their diseases, and any evil spirit within them came out, read Acts 19; 11 and 12. Therefore this Godly Michael believes that he is a man of God as well. It is a known fact that God will use whatever and whoever it takes to accomplish his will. Can you reach the mentally ill and the addict, well this mentally ill and addict person can.

There are some of God's people that have the same problems I have and this book will reach them and they will be saved. Life by Suicide has done that and will continue to do what it takes for people like my self to receive salvation. Those of us who suffer from all these illnesses need Life by Suicide to assist us in our road to recovery. As I told you earlier that we are damaged goods and need repair from the creator of live. All other things have failed us and we have grown weary and tired of trying just to fail. Therefore we now have Life by Suicide to guide us to our Lord and savior, in a way that only we can understand. As the Bible says nothing can keep us from the love of God. Neither can drugs and addictions. Nothing can!

I also understand that it is not God that does not love me. It is Satan the Devil and this world that hates me. Drug addicts have become more hated than discrimination and homosexuality. The drug addict is the most picked on people in society today. We are laughed at and made fun of on television. We are treated different in the court system that claims to be fair and uphold the law. And yet there are different laws for the same crime when you are an addict. I do understand this line of thinking. It is because we have taken so much from society with our selfishness and the willingness to do whatever it takes to get our drugs. I have heard of addicts killing their own parents for drug money. So I do understand, all is fair in love and war. However not ever addict is a killer. Some of us are good people in a bad situation. Regardless of what the world and the Devil think Life by Suicide will deliver some of us from your grip of hate.

My Godly Michael will not allow me to remain in your laughter and to be the brunt of your jokes. I remember telling you this earlier you had better watch how you carry yourself. Because the same thing that will make you laugh will also make you cry. And while you think addiction is so funny don't slip into the future and find yourself in the grips of addiction. I know you have no idea what that means so for your sake I will explain it to you. In other words don't let your future punish you for your past behaviors.

We never know what is going to happen in our lives. For one example don't let that son or daughter that you love so much die. And the pain is so great that you can't cope with it. Therefore you have yourself a drink and you feel better because the alcohol has eased your pain. However when the alcohol wears off you return to your pain. So you have another drink and this cycle continues day after day. Now you are totally dependent on alcohol to ease your pain. Hello addict! So keep laughing yourself into the pain of your future because after all you deserve it, it is funny right!

I watched this well respected judge on television ball up a small piece of paper and throw it on the bench to see how this alleged crack addict would respond. And this judge just laughed because he thought that was funny. It was a very bad decision and it showed the lack of character at that time. It was insulting and belittling. You see this Godly Michael thinks like this, besides Jesus Christ there is no man in the position to judge another man. Just because you are a judge does not give you the right to belittle people. You are suppose to be following the law and make a decision based on the understanding of the law. Not laughing at people and belittling them. You see my Godly Michael believes that God loves me so much that after all that I have done wrong in my life he has allowed me to live. God loves me so much that he has sent me to treatment eight times. He has saved my life three times that I know of. He has sent his angels and they have called out my name to stop me right before the moment of death's impact. This Godly Michael knows that when God loves you and he has a plan for you nothing can stop it.

I am actually now proud to be who I am. Hell, I feel like Paul right now. Because God is finally bringing me into his will for me. Therefore keep laughing. I wonder how many pieces of paper were thrown at Noah when he was building the ark and everybody was laughing at him. Well they slipped into their future and I know you know what happened to them. I also wonder how many people were laughing at Lot's door when he lived in Sodom. Well regardless of the amount they didn't laugh to long. This is what I meant when I said that the world hates me but God loves me. God hates homosexuality and yet you support homosexuality even in your own church. God said not to make for yourself any images of anything to worship him. And yet you wear your gold cross around your neck. And then you have the nerves to build a gold or wooden cross and put it in what you calls God's house. God told you that he is a spirit and those worshiping him must do it in spirit alone. But yet you continue to wear your gold crosses with the excuse it's just an aid or reminder. And you have the nerves to judge some one else.

Now if you do not understand what I am saying after I have made it so simple. Realize that this book is for those that God wishes to bring to salvation and not those that think they are already saved. This book is for the sick not for those who are well. This book is for the people with a Godly heart and Godly intentions but yet struggle with their earthly addictions and sicknesses. You have the nerves to have bake sales and yard sales in the Lord's house, and some of you even gamble for money all in God's house and yet you have the nerves to judge. Is this not the same things that were going on in the Bible when Jesus threw out all those buying and selling out of God's temple, you need to read Matthew 21;12 and 13.

Some of your hearts have been hardened and you can not understand. But thank you for buying this book I will use the money to help the people that you laugh at. You know like the homeless man on the streets that you walk pass everyday and laugh at. You know the people that you feel that are lazy and won't go get a job. You know what I'm talking about those people that you feel just don't want to help themselves. Those people that you think are beneath you. The ones that have had some kind of major tragedy in their life, and you don't know about it. Because all you see is this homeless man, so you laugh. This is because you have no Godly conscious. All you can see is the worldly things. Let me give you a simple example of what I mean.

I live in a duplex and we both have our own garage. There are enough parking spaces to park six cars behind our home. I have been living here for eight years and have had at least eight neighbors. I have not owned a car since I have been living here. So every neighbor that I have had gets comfortable and come to believe that the parking lot is theirs. So that when someone comes to visit me and park in the lot they get mad. They have become so use to parking wherever they want to and allowing their family and friends to do the same. That they think the parking lot belongs to them. They sometimes have the nerves to knock on my door and ask me to have my company move their car. One of my neighbors even called the tow truck and had my visitors car towed without even checking with me. There was another neighbor that had two cars in the parking lot that were not even working. These cars had been taken up parking spaces for nine months. One day I was studying the Bible with someone and this neighbor was in the parking lot screaming about my friend's car in their space. And what made it so bad was that there was still three other spots where she could have parked.

These are all selfish and greedy people with no regards for anyone else but themselves. After all they have the whole parking lot because I don't own a car. There are no markers that separate individual spots. But yet these people never think about that. It never crosses their mind that I have a right to the parking lot too. They have no Godly conscious. They are completely concerned about self. Some of these people have even had the nerves to call my landlord.

My Bible study now parks in the front of my home. I told him that he does not have to do that because this is my home too. However, he said not to worry about it. It will keep the tension down and keep me at peace with my neighbor's. This is having a Godly conscious. Being willing to let things go, even when you have a right to them.

Please understand that I am not trying to judge anyone because I am the last person on earth that has a right to do that. However I am stating the facts. This Godly Michael keeps in mind that Jesus said get away from me I don't even know you. Therefore you keep laughing and treating people the way you have. And I will be leaving Egypt with your treasure. And that is the gospel according to Michael. Tell me! Are you still laughing?

It is my wish that everyone that reads this book get something out of it to help them with whatever struggles that they may have. I know that when it rains it rains on the good and the bad alike. We are all creatures of God and none of us are better than the other. We all have our faults and we have all done wrong. As the Bible says, there is no one good. I just hope and pray that God will deliver me from my addictions and my sickness. My only wish is to live some length of happiness while in this body. And too serve God's purpose for me. Even if I don't live in some length of happiness, while in this body. I wish and pray that God will grant me eternal life for the good I have done while in this body. My salvation depends on what I have done while in this body. Therefore, may God bless this book and all those who read it!

When I look at the different men in me I come to realize that they are not as powerful as I believed them to be. That is because I have exposed them now. And their power over me seems to be seeking to a lower level of existence. One of the greatest things that I learned while in treatment is that once our secrets are exposed they no longer haunt us. The pain of the shame is what keeps us suffering. But once we talk about the shame in the secret the shame lessens and the pain seems to go away. We have taken the power away from our shame by exposing it. This exposure allows us to free ourselves from our shame and we once again become comfortable with ourselves. Once we are comfortable we can begin to work on whatever problem it is that we have. Life by Suicide will allow you to talk about that shame and free yourself. Life by Suicide teaches you that there is only one God and he already knows about your shame. So therefore you don't have to feel shameful when you go to him. God is the only person that can free us. Mankind has no power to do that so what they think really does not matter. Listen if you go to God with your problems and believe in your heart that he will deliver you then your hopes will become your reality.

The Bible says in the book of Matthew chapter 10 verses 28-31 "Don't be afraid of those who want to kill you. They can only kill your body; they cannot touch your soul. Fear only God, who can destroy both body and soul in hell. Not even a sparrow, worth only a half a penny, can fall to the ground without your father knowing it. And the very hairs on your head are all numbered. So don't be afraid; you are more valuable to him than a whole flock of sparrows". So you see that there is nothing about you that God doesn't already know. I know that it can be very hard because of the things that we have done. As well as how we feel about ourselves, but just go to God and he will heal you.

When I relapsed I felt so bad about myself and I felt terrible that I had let God down once again. My old thinking started to take over and I found myself slipping back into my old world of darkness. My Godly Michael was ministering to me everyday fighting off depression and my alcoholic Michael. He also had to fight off addiction to drugs and my mental health Michael's. And this took some time; at one point I had not written on my book for three weeks. But my Godly Michael kept fighting for me and I began to remember that nothing can keep us from the love of God. Then I slowly began to pray again. Sometimes I would not say one word while on my hands and knees praying. It was so hard to go back to God as a failure again. So the words just would not come out of my heart. But God knew my thoughts and he felt my pain because I am worth more to him than a flock of sparrows. And the very numbers of hair on my head he knows. My strength grew more and more every day. Then I once again was given salvation; through God's undeserved kindness. So please don't give up.

Life By Suicide

One of the saddest things I have ever seen in my life is a crack baby. At no fault of their own they are addicts and more than likely will have health problems as well as mental health issues. I have watched these small and sickly babies fight for their life with every breath they could mustard up. Their small and frile chest just pumps up and down with every struggling breath. You can see the pain and suffering that they are going through with every breath. My point is that with every breath we to have to struggle and fight for our lives. We must not allow our sicknesses to stop us from receiving our salvation.

We actually have a lot in common with these crack babies. Because of no fault of their own they have inherited these diseases from their drug addictive parents. We too through no fault of our own have inherited these imperfect bodies and sins from our disobedient parents. Our sicknesses were also handed down to us through our parents. We inherited death and all that goes along with it from our sinful parents. Adam and Eve have left us with addictions and mental health problems. Depression is a symptom of sin. So are all the other things that we suffer in these bodies from gambling addictions to Aids. Every problem they mankind has we have inherited from our forefather and fore mother.

So don't be too hard on yourself when it comes to going to God. God already knows our situation and is waiting for us to come to him. He has prepared a way for us already through his son Jesus Christ. Therefore there is no reason for us to be afraid to go to God. You see that your fleshly ways were inherited through Adam. But we have been saved through Jesus Christ. So even though we inherited death from Adam, we also have inherited life from Jesus Christ. With this new life we can rid ourselves of death and the symptoms that go along with it. Life by Suicide is just a plain and simple way of one mans struggle to rid himself of Adam's death grip. It is one man's way of seeking a new life through Jesus. I died through Adam but I live through Christ. You see somewhere in the blood line of all these great prophets of God's. Read Luke 3; 23-38! At some point if this blood line continued it would read Napoleon was the son of John Scott. And Michael was the son of Napoleon. So when I said to you that I believe I am just as good as these other men, this is also what I meant.

The bible says in the book of James chapter five verses seventeen and eighteen "Elijah was as human as we are, and yet when he prayed earnestly that no rain would fall, none fell for the next three and half years! Then he prayed for rain, and it poured down. The grass turned green and the crops began to grow". So learn from this example that you to are the child of God. And let no one tell you any different. Pray and pray and then pray some more. Don't let anything or anyone keep you from the love of God. There is no one that is good, not one. We have all sinned and fall short of the glory of God. So today it is through this blood line that I will no longer during the duration of this book call myself an addict or alcoholic. These people lived through Adam and these Michael's died through Jesus Christ. I am also a man of God. My faith in my lord and savior has given me my life back through his sacrifice on the torture stake for my sins. Today I am in recovery, the alcoholic and the drug addict was buried in Christ. And in the next upcoming chapter we will have a funeral for them.

I am telling you now that the Michael you meet at the beginning of this book is dead. I told you and now you have my promise that God will give you your salvation through your belief in his son Jesus Christ. I started off this book as the only hope to live. I literally wanted to kill myself, however because I loved my daughter so much I couldn't leave her in this world by her self. Therefore Life by Suicide was created. And now some of these Michael's are dead! There was some fasting and a lot of praying involved but Life by Suicide has killed off the old me from Adam and the new Michael is growing up and becoming alive through Jesus Christ.

Let no one belittle you or tell you that you are not worthy of God's love. If nothing else remember that these are the same people that threw pieces of paper and rocks at our lord Jesus Christ on his way to the torture stake. Show your love by following Jesus example and say for your own salvation, God forgive them for they know what not they do. And once again this is the gospel according to Michael. Let no one tell you that you are fat. That you are a drug addict! Let no one tell you that you can't eat this or that. From this day forward let no one tell you that you are worthless. You are a person of God the creator of all things. When people talk about you feel good about yourself because they also talked about the son of God. These are the ones that the Bible says that they keep turning themselves into angels of light. And it is no wonder because their father the Devil turns into an angel of light.

When Jesus Christ came back to life and his disciples had been fishing all day. They had caught nothing, not even one fish. He told them to throw their nets on the right side of the boat. Now he could have said throw your nets on the left side or even the front or back of the boat. No! He said on the right side of the boat. This was a parable for us to get on the right side of the lord. Right means the opposite of wrong. So live your life on the right side of the boat.

Once his disciples threw their nets on the right side of the boat they caught so many fish they could not even pull the net to shore. Make sure that you throw you net on the right side of the boat. Make sure that you live your life on the right side of the boat. It was no different when Jesus talked about the using of the seed of the fields. He was not literally talking about the seeds of the field. He was talking about the word of God. I tell you unless you believe in the lord Jesus Christ you can not be saved. Everything that Jesus did had some kind of meaning to it. He did not waste any time doing and saying things that had no meaning. Through prayer and fasting we learn the true meanings of his teachings.

My Michael's are being killed off through prayer and some fasting and with my confessions through this book. This is what they call the fourth step in Alcohol Anonymous having made a fearless and searching moral inventory of ourselves. Because of my degree of sickness my fourth step turned out to be a book. Therefore even though I have been sick, I now live. This is the essence of Life by Suicide. It is time to move on to the next chapter. I hope and pray that you have gotten something out of this book so far

Chapter Eight
General Hates and Core Beliefs

This chapter is about the many things that we believe in that are not good for our souls. Sometimes we have a lot of beliefs about things and people that are not true. In this chapter I will be talking about my beliefs in such things. This chapter is important because these are things that we don't believe have any effect on our lives. However, they do and it can also keep us from the love of God. Because God is love and there is no hate in him and if we are to go to God for our salvation we need to cleanse ourselves.

The belief that I have that is at the top of my list is police officers. I hate these people with a passion. It does not matter to me what color their skin is. If they are police officers I hate them. I believe that the only good cop is a dead cop. Don't stop reading now, remember that I told you that I am committing suicide in order for me to live. This conversation that we are engaged in is necessary for me to truly die. I also told you that I would not hold anything back to please my reader's. This is a legitimate hate for me and I must rid myself of it. I have always believed that all police are criminals with a badge. They are legal gang members with the law behind them. They can do whatever they want to and are held responsible by other members of their gang.

Listen, I am a Black man and all the police do is harass Black men through racial profiling. They come to court and lie about what actually happened. And once again I am not writing what I think, but what I have lived. Man I can't stand police officers. I am actually getting upset right now just expressing my feelings. There is an anger coming over me at this very moment. That shows you how much I hate these people with everything in my body.

You might be thinking that since I am or have been a criminal that is where my hate is coming from, but that is not it. My hate for these people goes deeper than that. I still recall the the images during the civil rights movement how they forced their dogs to attack Black people and sometimes even killed us. I still see today how they shoot Black men in the back eight times and call it justified. How can shooting someone in the back be justified? When you are looking at someones back they are retreating. There is no aggression towards you while looking at someones back. Looking at ones back means that they are leaving. There is no justification for shooting someone in the back. Just as there is no reason for a man to put his hands on a woman, except when his life is truly being threaten. There is also no reason whatsoever for shooting someone in the back. And this is actually ironic because as I am writing my T.V is playing in the background and the F.B.I is investigating the Minneapolis gang task force.

It is on the evening news here in Minneapolis, that these police officers were raiding drug houses and keeping the drug money for themselves. These police were taking from the drug houses big screen TV's and taking them home to their own families. They were taking ski jets and other valuable goods and keeping these things for themselves. What these officers did was nothing less than home invasion. And it was armed robbery because they drew their guns and took these things by force. The city of Minneapolis broke up the gang task force by sending each police officer involved to different sheriffs and police departments. And that is because like I said there is no one holding police responsible for their actions. Why would one gang member punish another gang member for something that they did to some one that is not in their gang? These police should be in jail and not working for another precinct.

You might think that they made a mistake and everyone makes mistakes every now and then. Well if anybody and I mean anybody can show me one good cop, just one. I'll be happy, but you can't do it because there is no such thing as a good cop. This was no mistake it was arm robbery and home invasion with intent to do bodily harm.

They appear to be people that while in childhood were cowards. And they grew up with an attitude and became police officers with a hate for others. Actually I really don't know any Black people that do like police. And why should we! All they do is kill our children and harass us with every opportunity they get. I have watched these people lie like dogs in the courtrooms of America. Swear to God that they are telling the truth and know that they are lying. Now if a criminal lies in the courtroom that is what you expect. However, it is totally different when someone who claims to be a representative of the law and of righteousness, that changes everything. These people are just as unrighteous as the criminals they arrest. But yet they are looked up to by most of society. They go home to their families as though they are heroes, and respected members of the community. But in all actuality they are no more than gang members with a badge.

I remember going to court for some crimes that I had committed. And the sheriffs were bringing me from the jail to the courtroom. I saw and heard the prosecutor and police officers trying to convince a witness to identify me as the person who had committed the crime. Although I had committed several crimes in which I was going to court for, this crime that they were talking about, I had not committed. As we were walking to the courtroom they were asking the witness was I the person that had robbed them. The witness said no, that is not the same man that robbed me. I told the sheriffs that were walking with me to look and listen to that. I told them that what they are doing is illegal. As we continued to walk towards them the witness said once again, that is not the man that robbed me. The police stated to the witness that this man is being charged with five other counts of robbery so help us get this nigger off the streets and say that he is the person that robbed you. I then turned to the two sheriffs that were on both sides of me and asked them did they just hear what the police said. They told me to keep walking and shut up. I told my attorney the whole story of what had just happened. Both sheriffs denied that they heard any of this and so did the police officer that said it and the prosecutor.

However, when this witness took the stand to testify against me he told the judge that his conscious was bothering him because of a conversation he had in the hallway with the police and prosecutor. The judge asked him to explain and he did. The judge dismissed the jury and was extremely upset with the police as well as the prosecutor. Therefore this charged against me was dropped. The prosecutor and the police received no disciplinary action for their behavior. A criminal is anyone who breaks the law and that is exactly what they did and yet nothing was ever done about it. Even the two sheriffs that was with me lied, and said they never heard the conversation. And after the judge dismissed the charge against me and I was on my way back to jail. I told them that they knew they heard the police try to convince the witness to identify me, they laughed and said so what, you got away anyway, so be happy.

I could go on and on about dishonest police but they are not my focus here. My focus is to rid myself of this hate for them. This hate for them literally eats at my very soul! Every time I see a police this hate appears and the terrible thing about this is that I live directly across the street from the police union. And there are always police there. It is very hard for me to enjoy my front patio without this hate appearing.

What I have decided to do is to pray and ask God to rid me of this hate. I can no longer live with this kind of hate anymore than I can live with alcohol and drugs. My God requires me to rid myself of the things that defile me and this is one of those things. I will even go on record at this point and say there might be such a thing as a good cop. And the only reason that I am willing to say that is because I am pretty sure that God has some of his people in that profession, maybe. However I will do all that I can to rid myself of this hate. And I'll tell you something else Black police officers are worse than the white ones.

However my only reason for this conversation is to rid myself of hate. And not to talk about how this systems works or for that matter who works in it. My happiness and salvation depends on how I live my life while in this body. So far I have not done such a good job, but through the undeserved kindness of God I still have time to change that. Therefore I repent and work towards my salvation by any means necessary. Nothing will get in the way of my happiness and this hate for police is not of God's will. So with that said and done I will move on to the next general hate for me.

At the very beginning of this book I stated that I was tired of everything and everybody, but mostly I am tired of myself. Most days before I even get out of bed I am already angry. I am already upset with myself and therefore everyone that I come into contact with is affected. I am not a pleasant person to be around most of the time. No one can attest to that more than my daughter. She is always asking me, why are you always mad? While like I tell her since I am so unhappy with myself it is only natural that I am mad all the time. Where does all of this anger come from? I will only assume that number one it would originate from my separation from God. The true source of my happiness. As I said earlier having been similar to a crack baby, and inheriting my fore- farther sin. I am naturally unhappy at birth. Add the drugs and alcohol, along with the depression and mental illnesses. There is no room for peace within me. My whole life has been torment within it's self. Also walking this earth alone is one of the worst things in the world. Being without family for the many decades that I have takes a toll on a man's soul. You become void and non- trusting to anyone. You learn to survive with just yourself and you depend on no other sources for your love. So you have no one to love and no one to love you, but you. This is the beginning of your; my in life. It becomes natural and it seems normal but you live your life with something always missing. A hole is created in your spirit and you try and fill emptiness with whatever you can find to make you feel better. For me that was drugs and alcohol along with sex and food. But the hole is never filled up because it is not the source of the emptiness. And you are angry all the time due to the lack of fulfillment.

And regardless of how hard you try that hole never shrinks nor does it fill up. So you continue to take in outside material to fill up a spiritual hole. The two will not mix and you continue in your own anger and unhappiness.

Now Life by Suicide has taught me to love myself by ridding myself of all things that defile me. Once I went to God with a humble heart and mind. It has taught me to surrender all things to him. And it has let me move out of my way and allow God to work in my life. The fact of the matter is I have always tried to fill this hole and have never been able to do it. So now I have gone to the repair shop for professional help. God created me, therefore he knows exactly what belongs in that hole. And with his guidance my hole is now shrinking. With God's help I have found the true meaning of sobriety and the source of staying free from drugs and alcohol. I now take my medications and that helps my mental illnesses which balances the chemicals in my brain and allows me to think positive about myself. I also talk with my family a lot more than I ever have in my life and have even thought about moving back home to be closer to them. In order for me to go back to Gary, that alone would be an act of God.

However, the anger in me is slowly quieting down and the hole is slowly being filled. My God has shown me the way to seek my salvation and to find some happiness on earth while still in this body. Through the grace of God Life by Suicide has given me that opportunity to look at myself honestly and do something about those things that have cheated me out of my happiness and my relationship with God. It has always been my intentions that when this book is completed, I would be free from the sources of myself. I would no longer be the man that I am and that a new Michael would be alive through the death of the old Michael. The very title of this book explains its purpose; Life by Suicide. And I will tell you this that there has been many tears and feelings involved in this process. Sometimes I have cried in front of other people.

I have a group of women that I became close to when I took their anger management course. I was exposing myself during the period when I relapsed. And this guy that works there was telling me not to be so hard on myself. He was encouraging me to my face and yet later I heard that he was laughing and talking about me to some other people. I talked about this earlier that it would not be wise of anyone to take my pain and make fun of it. This book is being blessed by God and to mock me is to mock the source of this book. The word God has been used over and over in this book therefore be careful with your laughter. The same things that will make you laugh will also make you cry. Also have you ever taken your garbage out and that smell of the garbage was with you until you dropped it in the garbage can. Well depending on how far your garbage can is from your home that smell could last forty five seconds to two minutes.

When you take my spiritual pain around with you it could last some time and even become a part of you. Please understand that I am trying to get rid of my demons. And rather you believe it or not they are looking for another soul to take over spiritually. So you don't want to carry my garbage too far or you might find yourself occupied.

I recall reading in the Bible where Jesus healed this man that had several demons in him. And the demons asked please don't kill us but let us go into that herd of pigs, and Jesus allowed them to flee into the herd. Please don't be the herd of pigs and run over the cliff and die. What more can I say about my anger. I actually prayed for this guy later. The Bible says "and don't sin by letting anger gain control of you. Don't let the sun go down while you are still angry, for anger gives a mighty foothold to the devil". So therefore anger is another thing that keeps me from my salvation.

Another one of my general hates and core beliefs is relationships with women. First of all I would like to say that I have no idea what a good woman is. I have never experienced the company of a good woman. It is mostly because I have chosen my women through unhealthy eyes. Because, I was so sick with my own illnesses that there is no way I could have chosen anything but trash. However, I have been cheated on and voodooed by women that I cared about. That's right this one woman actually voodooed me, seriously. This woman put a spell on me because I left her. And after seeing doctor's that had no idea what was going on. I was forced to go back to her, and she took the spell off of me. This woman put a hole inside my inner thigh and testicles the size of a golf ball. It was not bleeding or anything, it was just there. I could actually put three fingers into the hole. And the terrible thing about this is that she told me that she was going to do it if I ever thought about leaving her.

At that time in my life I never believed in voodoo or any of that kind of stuff. I always thought that you had to believe in that in order for it to work. However, I found out that is not true. The very next day after I left this woman this hole appeared out of nowhere. The doctor's didn't know what it was. I remembered she had told me what she would do to me if I ever left her. I, therefore called her and asked her, what have you done to me? And she said, what are you talking about? That hole in your ass. She then told me that I could never leave her and that hole would remain there until I came back home to her.

A friend told me that his mother was a practicer of voodoo and that she could help me. After having me sit in the bath tub with some herbs and other solutions that she had made up. She told me that whoever put this spell on you is the only person that can take it off. She told me that this person had been setting me up for years, and that for somebody to have that kind of control over my body, I had to have been eating her body fluids for years. She told me that this woman had been mixing her urine in my food, along with the blood from her period for years to have that kind of control over my body. She stated that she had to have hairs from my private parts as well as some of my semen. The fact of the matter is that this hole did not go away until I went back to this woman. The very next day the hole was gone and there was not even a scar there. You could not tell that it was ever there. I have not been the same man since when it comes to relationships. Furthermore I believe that women are helpers to mankind and that while they are equal to us in every way. They should know their rightful place. And there is nothing wrong with that statement, because at the same time men should also know their rightful place.

We are a unit and we work best as a team or a unit. When one part of that unit works outside of its boundaries then the whole unit become off balance. Understand that it is not my wish or intentions here to bash women or belittle them. They are just as important to this world and God's plan as man is. However to me women have lost what the significants of what a woman is. They are controlling and man is so weak that he has allowed it. They have become the head of the house hold and that is not God's plan for them.

I was volunteering at this local food shelf and this couple came in for some bread. The lady looked around and found the bread that she wanted. The husband or boy friend picked up the bread that he wanted and all that you could hear after that was her. She was telling him to put the bread back and that he did not need it. He said that he wanted it and that he was going to keep it. She continued to harass him about the bread. Asking him what are you going to eat that with and I already got the bread that we need. As I sat there watching this whole event unfold I remember saying to myself, that's why I am single. I will not and will I ever have a woman telling me what I can and can not do. As a grown man I will do what I want to do without some woman's two cents. There is nothing wrong with your wife asking you something, but don't tell me what I can't have and do. I watch some of my friend's wives just control their every move. They can't go here , they can't go there. I actually know some weak grown men that have curfews. And I call them weak because that is what they are. I attended a family violence class and there the teacher's were women.

Now I was court ordered there for hitting this women and choking her. I do not believe that a man should put his hands on a woman. However if it is to save his live or keep him from harm, so be it.

This woman had a butcher's knife and was trying to stab me and I don't care what you say or think I was not going to let that happen. And even though I graduated from that class I still believe in my heart that I did what I had to do in order to save myself from harm. Just because I am a man I suppose to let you cut me with a knife. However, there was a lot of drugs and alcohol involved. But the point is if you try and hurt me you can be cat, dog or woman I will protect myself. I teach my daughter to walk away from words and if at all possible stay away from fighting. But I also teach her that if somebody put their hands on you then you protect yourself by any means necessary. I tell her that I would rather visit you in jail than visit you at a funeral home. I learned a lot while in this family violence program but that is something I refuse to surrender to.

Anyway it is not a womans job to tell man what to do. A womans decision should not be the final say so. However, men these days are so weak that they allow this to happen. Men want the use of the woman's body so bad that they have compromised their manhood for sex. This within it's self is wrong. No woman should deny her husband sex and no man should deny his wife sex. Unless they both agree to spend that time worshiping God. You need to read 1 Corinthians 7; 3-5. It clearly states that "the husband should not deprive his wife of sexual intimacy, which is her right as a married woman, nor should the wife deprive her husband. The wife gives authority over her body to her husband and the husband gives authority over his body to his wife. So do not deprive each other sexual relations. The only exception to this rule would be the agreement of both husband and wife to refrain from sexual intimacy for a limited time to give themselves to prayer".

As I said earlier woman is also a part of God's plan. In the Bible book of 1 peter chapter three verse seven it says" in the same way, you husbands must give honor to your wives. Treat her with understanding as you live together. She may be weaker than you are, but she is your equal partner in God's gift of new life. If you don't treat her as you should, your prayers won't be answered". So the man is to treat his wife with honor and respect, she is not to control anything. Read the book of Ephesians chapter five verses twenty two through twenty five you will see the meaning of the womans will by God. It simply states that "you wives will submit to your husbands as you do to the Lord. For a husband is the head of his wife as Christ is the head of his body the church; he gave his life to be her savior. As the church submits to Christ, so you wives must submit to your husbands in everything".

However man is to love his wife as he loves himself. Man has lost the natural use of his body just as woman has. We have been given up to the Devil because of our sins. Men no longer follow God's will for them, and woman has taken over the role as the man. One of the things that truly get on my nerves is women that tell men they can't see their own children. And once again man is so weak and punk'd out that they allow it. What kind of woman would not want their child to know their own father? This is the Eve in this woman. And, what kind of man would allow a woman to stop him from seeing his own child? This is the Adam in these men. These are the same men that followed Eve when God told him not to disobey him. Just as Adam allowed Eve to stray him from righteousness. So has man today allow women to take over the role as the head of the house hold. It is not natural and that is why the divorce rate is so high.

Life By Suicide

That is why there is so much domestic violence and so many extra marital affairs.

I don't expect everyone that reads this book to agree with me and that's fine. However, read the scriptures for yourself and then you do whatever makes you happy. I am only fighting for my own salvation and if this is not a problem for you, then don't take it personal. If people would not listen to Jesus and his disciples I know you could care less about what I am saying. Therefore I will not go on and on. All of the sheep of the Lords will hear his voice and come to him. I am not the Lord, I am only doing the work of God in order to free myself from the grips of hell. Do as you please, but you won't be able to say that I didn't know. As I told you earlier there is no reason for not knowing God. He has made himself know from the beginnings of the world. The bottom line to this core belief for me is that I will allow God to choose my wife. Or I will remain single. But I need a wife for me to continue to be single means that I will be unable to have sexual relations. Although I will accept whatever situation that the Lord sees fit for me. If I get married fine and if I don't get married that's fine too.

My prayers in that case would be that God gives me the strength to refrain from sex. And I would definitely need God to refrain from having sex. So I wish to be married because sexual sins are against your own body. The Bible says "to run away from sexual sins! No other sin so, clearly affects the body as this one does. Sexual immortality is a sin; against your own body" 1 Corinthians 6; 18.

There are some other things that trouble me to my core. That is the way this system of things is set up in the United States. This only gets on my nerves because I have a lot of white friends. And I must say that White people think totally different from Black people. When it comes to how this government is seen our differences are as apart as our skin colors are. I have a lot of white friends and hopefully I still have them after they read this part of this book. However, I made a promise to myself that I would not hold anything back. Before I explain where I am going here, let me just say that if everybody in America got back on the boats that their ancestors came over here on. The only people that would be left are the Native

Americans, Indians. So now that I have gotten that out of the way, let me continue.

There is more America's than just white America. Just as there are many Michael's living in this one body. There are many other people living in America. You have Black America and you also have Mexican America. Then there is Indian America and so forth and so forth. The point is that America is a country full of immigrants, we all come from some place else. But the white man thinks that this is his country alone. He has the tendency to claim everything and is dishonest about most things. Regardless of the wrong involved he is always right in his mind. Out of his mouth comes the constitution of the United States but out of his heart comes, the Jim Crow and the slave owner mentality. Even in his right intentions he can not help but be greedy and hateful to all that is around him. He honestly believes that he is the superior race and that everybody else is here to do his will. In one hand he spreads his wealth all over the world helping poor countries and with the other hand he spreads his hate over the same world, just taking whatever he wants.

Today is September the 9th 2009 and when I started writing this part of my book it was September the 7th 2009. I knew that I had to write about this because it is one of the things that defile me. But at the same time I wanted to be sensitive to my friends and to my innocent readers. However, after watching the President of the United States address congress and the disrespect shown to Barack Obama I knew that being proud to be an American was a lie. First of all I know that this Black man could not have become president without the vote and help of many white people. So please don't misunderstand what I mean. However, Jim Crow, excuse me, I meant Congressman Joe Wilson had to show the true meaning of being White America. Even if that is the way he feels then it was a better place and time for his hate. First of all forget the fact that Obama is Black. What Congressman Joe Wilson did was totally disrespectful to the office of the President of the United States. He disrespected every one of his colleagues rather they be democratic or republican. He then disrespected every American citizen. His apology is unacceptable and should not be accepted.

As I watched the coverage afterwards not one news media representative spoke about his actions in the manner that they should have. It all goes right back to what I said earlier in this book, they are drug dealers covered up. Spitting their hate to all the world and contaminating all that they encounter. Congressman Joe Wilson's comment was also an insult to every Black man, woman and child in this country. The president of this country is Black. It was Black slaves that built the White House, so it's about time that we live in it. Our last president before Barack Obama lied to the American public over and over about this war in Iraq and not one republican said; you lie. Therefore what Congressman Joe Wilson was really saying is that I don't mind you lying to me about getting five thousand and counting American children killed through war. But I'll be damned if I will let you lie to me about saving Americans through health care. He was saying that I would rather keep my mouth closed about murder, but you try and save some ones live and I'll loose my temper. He was saying that I will disrespect my colleagues and this country along with the President of the United States if you try and save some ones life in front of me. Am I judging this man, no but what I am doing is explaining his actions and what they really meant.

This is where my hate for white people like him comes into my life. And this is what defiles me through that hate. As I said that I have a lot of white friends whom I love, therefore I am not talking about white people in general. I'm talking about the Jim Crows and the Joe Wilson's of this great country.

The man that I spoke about earlier in this book that gave me that car was white. The people that forgave me for robbing them and never told on me was white. The lady that gave me this computer that I am writing this book on is white. Also the man that delivered this computer and set it up at my desk is white. And I can write another book on how much love and help I have received from white people. There is no racism involved here, I am only speaking facts. As a matter of fact at this moment and time in my life the only friends that I do have are all white.

Let me close by saying once again I am ridding myself of all the things that defile me and this is one of those things. I will also say that I was born in this country and my father was born in this country, and his father before him and his father before him and his father before him and his father before him. So if you can't say the same thing, then if anybody needs to get back on the boat and go home it's you. As I said earlier the media or should I say the White media or drug dealers is just as racist as Jim Crow, excuse me once again I meant Congressman Joe Wilson.

One week later a Black music rapper interrupted a White country singer at the video music awards. And the media talked about him like he was a dog. He was called disrespectful and rude. He was called ignorant and stupid. He was the most hated Black man in America besides O.J Simpson for that one week.

Barack Obama as president can't really say how he feels because he is the president, and I don't know how he feels. However, I can say what I feel and know to be true. First of all there has been no greater president in this country in the last twenty years. And it dam sure was not Bush, son or father. You white people are just naturally hateful and there is nothing you can do to change that. It does not matter how hard you pray your hate is there. You think that you are superior, but you are not. You are nothing more than tools put in position by God to bring to him his true people. Your position in this country is the same as Egypt's Pharaoh was to the children of Israel. Therefore you too, will drown in the Red Sea.

It does not matter how great of a job President Obama does these White people will still spit their hate. These are the same people that supported every policy that our previous president asked for. The war in Iraq and Afghanistan, these are the people directly responsible for thousands of Americas children dying in a war that was a lie. These people are directly responsible for the crisis that this country is in at this very moment. From the housing crisis to health care, and yet you see these people on talk shows like they had nothing to do with it. That's the reason every time they open their mouth the rest of America see how stupid they really are. And yet they think that they are smart and wise, God has close their eyes and their minds, so they walk around proud in their stupidity. Not knowing that the communion they have been taken has left them weak and sick, and some have even died.

And last but not least my ridding myself of this is according to God's will. In the Bible book of Romans 13; 1 and 2 it says "obey the governments, for God is the one who put them there. All governments have been placed in power by God. So those who refuse to obey the laws of the land are refusing to obey God, and punishment will follow". Therefore since I seek my salvation through God I will obey the laws of the land. And just to exercise my Life by Suicide I will also pray for Congressman Joe Wilson, well I might be lying about that.

Now let me move on to another topic that also defiles me. I have a problem paying my debts. For so long the only person that I have paid back is the drug dealer. And the only reason he got paid was so I could get more drugs on credit when I needed it. When you owe some one that person owns a piece of you until that debt is paid. Why? Owing debt can be very stressful and belittling. There is something about owing some one that keeps you thinking about them until that debt is paid. Then when you have money and have to do something else with that money. You always end up thinking about that person that you owe. And it is in this sense that owing someone allows you to be owned.

Especially if you don't have the money and there are obligations that are more important to you. Owing people money causes a lot of problems. It causes us to loose friendships and relationships. Sometimes we even stay awake at night thinking about our debt. And once again in this sense owing somebody allows you to be owned. The pure pressure of not being able to pay your debt is within it self time consuming and stressful. Then comes the time when you see that person or they call you about their money. And you don't have it you become obligated to that person. You become a slave to the person that you owe.

My debt is terrible however the personal debt that I owe is not as bad as the general debt. I have been so sick that when the debt collectors call my home, I would just tell them the truth. I remember saying over and over to different debt collectors, that I am a drug addict and alcoholic. I don't have your money and more than likely when I do get some money. It will be going to the drug dealers and the liquor stores. And I doubt very seriously if you will see any of it.

But if you would like to call back to see if there is any money left, you are welcome. I know that is funny but it is the truth. Most of the time they would never call me back. And as far as my credit report is concerned when they threaten me with that, I just tell them to be my guest. And that they have no idea how long that line is.

However I am tired of being owned by my debts. I believe that if you owe somebody then you should pay your debts. For so long all my money went to drug dealers and the liquor stores and I didn't care about anything or anybody else. But now since I seek my salvation from God, it is my wish to learn how to do his will. And it is through this faith that I confess my sins, in hopes of a better life. You must keep in mind that these are the things that are keeping me from my salvation. You might be different and not as server as mine.

However whatever it takes to free ourselves from the grips of hell do it. Hell being the opposite of salvation, and not burning forever. From this point on I will make a clear and honest effort to pay off my debtors both personal and business. My goal here has not changed it is happiness that I seek. And that happiness comes through my salvation. Also keep in mind that these are the things that defile me, you are to use those things that defile you and keep you from your salvation.

I will move on to the next subject of my defilements. Lying is almost natural to me when it comes to something that I want. And for the last thirty five years all that I seemed to have wanted is drugs and alcohol. I have told so many lies to get these chemicals that I wouldn't even know where to start. I can however tell you this every member in my family has died more than once. My soul was consumed with lies and my mind was the creator of my lies. God does not like liars and I have been one for most of my adult life. I don't so much lie in general, but when it comes to trying to feed my addictions I tell lies ridiculously.

Lies can be very hurtful and even cause the death of some one. My salvation depends on me training myself to be honest. And I will need to train myself, because when you lie for so long it becomes natural. I don't lie just to lie, but for drugs, if I have robbed people before can you imagine my lies. I don't know how to tell you anymore than what I have said about lies. I don't know how someone else feels when they are lied to. But I know how I feel when I am lied to by someone that I trust.

I remember when I lived in Atlanta. I was dating this girl name Debra. Shortly after we had broken up I heard that she was pregnant with my child. Therefore I went to see her and she told me that it was true. However her mother was not going to allow her to have the baby, because she needed to finish school and go to college. Therefore she was having an abortion and wanted me to help pay for it. And that is what I did. The day she was suppose to have the abortion I called her and she said that her mother and her was leaving right then and for me to call her later. I waited until the next day before I called her back. She said that she had the abortion and that she was fine. After that conversation with her I did not see her for at least another four years.

When I saw her years later I was telling her how nice she looked. She told me not to talk to her. I asked her, what have I done to you? I told her that if this is about the abortion I never wanted that and that you and your mother controlled everything. I told her that it was never my wish and she knew that then. She then told me that since I was not man enough to take care of a baby that she had nothing to say to me. She then told me that she did not have an abortion and that she had the child. She refused to give me her phone number or her new address and said that I would never see my child. Until this day I still at least twice a year wonder if I have a child that I have never seen or known. I live with myself because I don't know if she lied about being pregnant or the abortion or even the child being born. I was nineteen then and in eleven days I will be fifty one years old and I still sometimes wonder.

All of the things that I am revealing in this book I am also praying about them. I need my salvation and I will not let anything stop me from receiving it. Lying can be very harmful and that is why I will continue to pray and ask God for his forgiveness so that I can find my happiness.

One other thing that defiles me is the lack of education. I believe that not having the proper education keeps a person from living a life full of hopes. When there is no education there is no power and when there is no power there is no voice. Without a voice you are not heard. And when you are not heard then you have no hope. No hope brings forth low self esteem which follows alcohol and drugs, over eating and depression. These are the very same things that defile us. So our education is just as important as any other thing that we have discussed. Without education you become a beggar. And the only hope that a beggar has is the hope to stand in state welfare lines. I have always been able to read and write, but there are no skills or career underneath that foundation.

So to get me out of this situation I have decided to take time out after I finish this book. And find out what it is I would like to do. I really believe that teaching the word of God is what I was put here for. Therefore I would have to rely on God, for he is the instructor of his word.

I could go on and on about things that defile me. However, I have told you and shown you the road in which you need to take. My job is done here and the things that have defiled me have been exposed. There are a few other minor things that I can handle in the privacy of my own life. Therefore it is time to have my funeral, so that I can rise up to life. For this is what Life by Suicide is all about. Killing off all the things that made me unhappy and failing to seek my salvation. I have done this throughout this book and the man that started writing this book is dead. Michael now lives through his faith in our Lord Jesus Christ. It is because of him that I have been granted immunity from my sins. And it is through him that I rise from the dead to the living. I have shredded off the Adam, Michael that is the fleshly Michael. And I have risen in the spirit of the Jesus, Michael.

However, there is one other thing I must do. That is to be baptized by spirit and water. For the Bible says that in order for a man to enter into the kingdom of God he must be born again. In the Bible book of John 3; 5 it states "Jesus replied, the truth is, no one can enter the kingdom of God without being born of water and spirit. Humans can reproduce only human life, but the Holy Spirit gives new life from heaven". So this is my last deed in order for Life by Suicide to be completed.

Chapter Nine
My Last Words

Everything that I have said in this book is true and has happened to me in this life. The things that I have told you were given to me to tell you. There is nothing in this book that I have lied about or misrepresented. There are somethings in this book that you might disagree with and that is your salvation, not mine. I have sought through prayer and meditation along with some fasting to see if there was anything that God did not want me to write. When my spirit was troubled I followed my spirit and did as it said.

For example when I first started this book I spoke against traditional treatment centers for drugs and alcohol. Then God showed me through my relapse that his hands created these anonymous groups. And what God has called clean let no man call dirty. Therefore I was forced to recall my statements about these treatment centers not working. Because God revealed to me that was not his will for this book. Whatever I have written in this book has been approved by my spirit and my relationship with God as I understand him. I have consistently given you Bible verses that you can read for yourself. I have explained to you over and over the things that are in this book. I have used my own personal experiences to show you the way and how it affects us as human beings. I have expose things that I have never told anybody. It was very painful and shameful to talk about the homosexual experience that happened in my life. However, my spirit and my relationship with God would not let me leave that out of this book. It was a vital part of ridding myself of the things that defile me.

Michael F. Clark

Life by Suicide calls for the brutal truth, therefore I had no choice. Furthermore, I will have to explain that to my daughter, she has no idea about that incident in my life. So if you think that I would not even spare her that pain, then know that I have not lied to you. I started off with suicidal thoughts. I had no idea that I was going to put my life in words for the world to read.

Life by Suicide was created to save my life and in the hopes that I could find my salvation. Life by Suicide was created to find me some length of happiness in my life. Life by Suicide was created because I did not want to kill myself literally and leave my daughter in this world by herself. Life by Suicide was created because after pretending to be dead for over thirty days I still used drugs and alcohol. Simply put, Life by Suicide was created as my last line of defense to fight for my salvation.

If there is something in this book that you disagree with, then take the things out of this book that you do agree with. Some events that are in this book I did not know would ever happen during the course of my writings. Things like seeing the first Black President of the United States, the death of Michael and that of Mr. Kennedy. These events were not of my doing. However, when they happened it was no doubt that they were to be a part of this book for the purpose of illustration only. When the President of the United States was disrespected by Congressman Joe Wilson. This happened at the very same time that my writings were talking about how white people think that they are better than the rest of mankind. As a matter of fact I stopped my writing because of all the white friends that I have. I wanted to make sure that no good white people were hurt by my statements and that it did not sound racist. It was during this break from my writings that this man in front of the whole world disrespected the president and this country. That was a force greater than myself telling me to continue with exactly what I was saying. It was a perfect example of what I was talking about. Therefore I continued.

Also my dislike for police, at the same time of my writing several Minneapolis police committed home invasions and robberies. Kept property that should have went to the evidence department. So rather you believe me or not, know this. These things were not simple coincidences, these things were meant for this book. And it was through no doing of my own.

I have quoted dates in this book so that you would know that you were witnessing a man committing suicide while writing about it. I first started writing on this book September the 30th 2008, it is now September 12, 2009, 10;38 am Saturday morning. It is eighteen days short of a full calendar year since I began killing myself. I could finish this book today, however I want to pray and maybe even fast about how to close my writings. I want to seek God's approval before I finish his work for me. I want to make sure that I have his blessings.

It is now 6;08 am Sunday morning, September 13, 2009 I have come to the conclusion that God's blessing are with me. And while I did not fast my prayers and my dreams were not interrupted. My spirit is comfortable to close out this book. Some things like going to heaven and hell are things that you have believed all of your life. But one of the Devil's greatest weapons is false religion. And when we believe that God has made mistakes that is a false teaching. The Bible book of Isaiah 45; 18 says in The New Living Translation"for the lord is God, and he created the heavens and the earth and put everything in place. He made the world to be lived in, not to be a place of empty chaos". Then in the New World Translation Isaiah 45;18 says " for this is what Jehovah has said, the creator of the heavens. He, the true God, the former of the earth and the Maker of it, He the one who firmly established it, who did not create it simply for nothing, who formed it even to be inhabited. I am Jehovah and there is no one else".

So when we believe that God created this earth for nothing then we believe false teachings. You can no more worship God from a power base of false teaching than you can bring a child into this world with two men. It is just not possible. And the same thing goes for hell. God is love and would no more burn you forever and ever. This is the teachings of the Devil, the one who is misleading the entire earth. There is no more that I can say about this you are on your own. You will either believe what the Bible says or you will believe what the Devil says. Hopefully you read your Bible and pray for your own understanding. This is where working and fighting for your salvation comes into play. Either way my work is done here. Life by Suicide has done exactly what it was created for. And that was to give me a fighting chance for my salvation.

I will end this book by stating the words of the first Black President of the United States. I can now live up to the full measurement of my happiness thanks to almighty God and his son Jesus Christ, whom through undeserved kindness, Life by Suicide was created.